YOUR GUIDE TO THE JEWISH HOLIDAYS

YOUR GUIDE TO THE JEWISH HOLIDAYS

FROM SHOFAR TO SEDER

CANTOR MATT AXELROD

JASON ARONSON
Lanham • Boulder • New York • Toronto • Plymouth, UK

Published by Jason Aronson
A wholly owned subsidiary of Rowman & Littlefield
4501 Forbes Boulevard, Suite 200, Lanham, Maryland 20706
www.rowman.com

10 Thornbury Road, Plymouth PL6 7PP, United Kingdom

British Library Cataloguing in Publication Information Available

Library of Congress Cataloging-in-Publication Data
Axelrod, Matt, 1966– author.
   Your guide to the Jewish holidays : from shofar to Seder /
cantor Matt Axelrod.
      p. cm.
   Includes index.
   ISBN 978-0-7657-0989-9 (cloth : alk. paper) —
   ISBN 978-0-7657-0990-5 (electronic)
   1. Fasts and feasts—Judaism. I. Title.
BM690.A84 2014
296.4'3—dc23
                                                    2013033886

Printed in the United States of America

For Judah and Josh

CONTENTS

ACKNOWLEDGMENTS

THE BOOK that you're holding in your hands is the end result of a long process that could never have taken place without the hard work and professional expertise of a bunch of people. First, I'd like to thank my agent, Anne Devlin, for her constant effort and wise advice. Thank you to the wonderful folks at Jason Aronson, and especially Lindsey Porambo and Julie Kirsch, for their tireless work at turning my thoughts and sometimes questionable attempts at humor into a coherent and readable manuscript.

I'm enormously grateful to my friends and congregants at Congregation Beth Israel in Scotch Plains, New Jersey, for always showing their warmth and support. It's been an honor and a pleasure to call our temple my family's home for so many years. Finally, this book could never have been possible without the ever-present love and patience of my wife, Tali, and sons, Judah and Josh. Thanks for making this so much fun.

INTRODUCTION

O H GREAT, just what the world needed—another book about the Jewish holidays.

If you're like a lot of people, your basic understanding of every Jewish holiday consists of "They tried to kill us. We won. Let's eat."

There always seems to be another arch villain who has it out for the Israelites, at which point God intervenes, the dastardly plot is foiled, and we can all happily sit down to our traditional festive meal of gefilte fish, potato latkes, and grape juice (the three items that each supermarket puts on sale for *every Jewish holiday*).

If you attended a synagogue religious school many years ago, you may have learned a little more about the holidays. Then you proceeded to learn the exact same thing every single year after that. When a second grader asks why we do certain things for each holiday, you can get away with answering, "Because it's in the Torah and God told us to." Unfortunately, that's still the answer that a lot of adults get when they reasonably ask the same question later in life.

Consider this book the response to all that. Inside, you'll find all the stuff you never learned in Hebrew school. For instance, how many New Years are there in the Jewish calendar? Why is there absolutely no mention of any oil or a miracle in the original Chanukah story? What makes the fun, kid-friendly Purim story of Esther and Mordechai one of the bloodiest and most violent books of the Bible?

I've found that most books about Judaism read like a dry instruction manual: "Place menorah on the table. Carefully insert the proper number of regulation-sized Chanukah candles in menorah. Light the candles and say the mandated blessings." Other times, when you ask a question, the answers themselves make you even more confused because they're filled with terms and phrases that people assume you should already know. And that in turn makes you afraid to ask anything else. Finally, a lot of books and material on the Jewish holidays are heavily laden with religious overtones, implicitly judging you for not being more observant and failing to provide any information for the casual reader who's simply looking to learn more, even in a secular environment.

It's time to bring these holidays to life and learn about them in an enjoyable way, with accessible explanations and interesting and useful facts, along with a generous dose of humor.

This book is perfect for you if

- you always wanted a better understanding of the Jewish holidays but had no idea where to start and were afraid to ask someone and risk listening to a boring answer for two hours.
- you remember the same tired facts from Hebrew school but want to learn about the holidays on an adult level.
- you know that Jews are *supposed* to observe the holidays but want to know what makes the holidays relevant in modern times.
- you are a non-Jewish person who is seeking to find out much more about the Jewish holidays and rituals. Maybe you're in the process of embracing the Jewish religion on your own, or are embarking on a relationship with someone who is Jewish, and you want a more thorough understanding of the festivals and occasions.

There are also sections within each chapter marked "In Depth," or "Perfect for Families" that delve into the material in different ways. You'll read about every holiday's back story, which provides the proper context for each occasion's existence and traditions. And you'll have a chance to discover more modern interpretations and customs.

Of course, what would the Jewish holidays be without food? I'll explain some of the common foods associated with the festivals (hint: gefilte fish is not mentioned in the Torah even once) and why they've become traditional.

You can easily read this book cover to cover and really appreciate the cycle of the Jewish calendar and see how each holiday, with its distinct mood and emotions, flows into the next. Alternately, feel free to simply turn to a certain chapter if you're interested in finding out more about a specific holiday. I also include a guide at the end of the book that briefly summarizes the main points of each holiday, but don't even think about skipping the entire book and just reading that first. That would be cheating.

Get ready to explore the beauty and meaning of the Jewish holidays.

CHAPTER 1

ROSH HASHANAH

REPENT NOW!

W HEN IS a new year not a new year?

The idea of celebrating a new year, the change in the calendar from the end of one year to the first day of the next one, is something we can all understand. In our own Gregorian calendar (which I like to call the "regular calendar" for the sake of simplicity), the concept is neat and tidy. Each year we come to the end of December, gather with friends, and fight to stay awake until the magic hour of midnight, at which time we wish each other "Happy New Year!" and hastily make our exits so we can get home and in bed by 12:03 a.m.

Shouldn't it be that easy in Judaism?

Rosh Hashanah, which means "head of the year," is the Jewish New Year. The new year of our regular calendar predictably takes place on the first day of the first month (January 1). Similarly, we would assume that the Jewish New Year falls on the first day of the first month of the Jewish calendar. Since the Hebrew date of Rosh

Hashanah falls on the first day of Tishrei, that all seems to work out fine. But Tishrei is not the first month of the Jewish calendar. It's really the seventh month. That's right, the Jewish New Year falls on the first day of the *seventh* month.

The Torah does not mention months by name, but rather gives them numbers: the first month, the second month, and so on. If that's the case, then how can we be sure that Tishrei isn't the Torah's first month? In fact, the first month is counted from the exodus from Egypt, something that we'll talk all about when we get to the chapter on Passover. That holiday, of course, takes place in the spring, and occurs in the Hebrew month of Nisan. Therefore, the Torah considers Nisan to be the first month, making Tishrei the seventh month. That's like celebrating New Year's Day on July 1. Why do we have such a strange quirk of timing in the Jewish calendar?

The Back Story

There is no mention of a holiday having to do with a new year or anything called "Rosh Hashanah" in the Torah.

However, we do read in the book of Leviticus that the first day of the seventh month will be a holy day, when we should hear the blowing of horns. We're not supposed to do any work on this day, the usual command for the Jewish holidays that are considered sacred. I tried using that line when I asked to take a vacation day on Rosh Hashanah one year. (It didn't work.)

That's it. That's the Torah's treatment of this mysterious, not-yet Jewish New Year. Later in the book of Numbers we read about specific sacrifices that were brought on this and other holidays. Not only is there no mention of any New Year, but, in fact, no reason is given at all for this holiday other than the date on which it falls, and the fact that it's a sacred day.

It wasn't until many centuries later, in the time of the Mishnah (around the first century), that we come across the term "Rosh Hashanah" for the first time. The ancient rabbis took this sacred occasion, characterized by the blowing of a horn and taking place on the first day of the seventh month, and turned it into a New Year's celebration.

In effect, they created a second new year, based on different ways of looking at the calendar.

There's a good reason why the rabbis did this. As we go through many of the holidays in this book, we'll see that they often revolve around the agricultural cycle of the year—planting, rainy season, harvest, and so on. The autumn was the time of year when this cycle would come full circle. It was the end of the summer heat, the beginning of the rainy season when the success of the crops would be most at risk, and a time to harvest that which was planted before. Regardless of whether people observed any religion, it felt very much like a new year.

You can easily understand how they viewed this cycle because most kids feel the same way in modern times as they all head back to school each autumn and begin a new year. Since the school calendar hearkens back to a pre-industrial, agricultural time, it's certainly no accident that both Rosh Hashanah and the first day of school fall around the same time of year.

So while there was still a "biblical" year that had Nisan as the first month, the rabbis gave us another way to look at the calendar, through an agricultural perspective, which now had Tishrei as the beginning.

The Back Back Story

Some important themes of Rosh Hashanah actually come from outside the Jewish tradition. In Babylonian times, pagan cultures would commonly celebrate a festival in which their own gods were enthroned. They worshipped many deities and idols, so they figured that some must be more powerful than others. As a result, it made sense to stage a coronation for their most powerful god or gods, and then the people and the other, lesser gods would pledge to serve them. Like other pagan festivals, this revolved around the cycle of farming and climate. It was logical to schedule this kind of commitment to the god-king around the most vital and vulnerable time of year, when they were hoping for rain and a good harvest.

This theme of enthronement was the basis for what became Rosh Hashanah. In order to both lure ancient Jews away from pagan rituals and to emphasize that God (the big guy with a capital *G*) was the one, true king over everything, the rabbis imbued Rosh Hashanah, the Jewish New Year, with themes of enthronement and God's sovereignty.

Double Down

Wouldn't it be more enjoyable for New Year's Day to last *two days?* Sure, let's make the holiday fall on January 1 and 2. There's no doubt that some people could use the extra day to recover from their parties.

That's exactly what we do for Rosh Hashanah. The Jewish New Year occurs on the first and second days of Tishrei.

Rosh Hashanah, like a lot of the other holidays mentioned in the Torah that we'll learn about throughout this book, is actually observed one extra day. Indeed, the Torah only says that we should set aside the first day of the month as a sacred day. It doesn't say anything about the first and second days.

This practice originated in ancient times before everyone had a reliable calendar hanging in their kitchen. Back then, the best way to keep track of the passage of time was simply by looking at the moon. Since the Jewish calendar is lunar (that is, the months correspond directly to the cycle of the moon), it became fairly easy to figure out when holidays took place. It's for this reason that the vast majority of Jewish holidays and festivals take place on either the first of the month, when there would be a new moon, or the fourteenth or fifteenth of the month, during a full moon.

Still, even something as seemingly obvious as a new moon had to be verified and agreed upon. So observers would stare into the night sky, and as soon as someone viewed the new moon, they would report to the Sanhedrin, the local council of Jewish authorities. The Sanhedrin, in turn, would make sure that the observer's testimony was reliable and accurate. If they were satisfied, they would declare, "New Moon!"

It would take some time for the Sanhedrin's declaration to make it out to far-flung areas. In the interest of making sure that Jews would observe holidays on the right day even if they hadn't received the news yet, the ritual of making a holiday last two days became the norm. That way, even if the news of the new moon came late, they were covered.

Since we can now pinpoint every moment in the calendar with perfect accuracy in perpetuity, you're probably wondering why we still observe some holidays for two days. After all, we can tell to the second when the new month of Tishrei begins.

The answer lies in a rabbinical precept in which Jews strive to increase the number of holy things they do, not reduce the number. Since those extra days were already added, it would seem wrong if we took holy days away from the Jewish calendar. It also proves extremely effective for a typical family to avoid a huge fight and have two Rosh Hashanah dinners, one with each side of the family.

Some Jewish communities, especially in the Reform movement, have in fact made the change to one-day observances of some holidays. Interestingly, even among those synagogues that have switched to celebrating other holidays for only one day, some may still observe Rosh Hashanah for the traditional two-day duration.

Rosh Hashanah, along with the very important next holiday of Yom Kippur, is commonly referred to as one of the High Holidays, or, in Hebrew, *Yamim Noraim*, the Days of Awe.

Pay to Pray?

During the High Holidays, synagogues see their highest attendance numbers of the year. A temple that might see twenty, thirty, or even a hundred worshippers on a normal Saturday morning has to utilize every nook and cranny, open every folding door and wall, and set up hundreds of folding chairs in order to accommodate their entire membership as well as their family members. It's a *lot* of people crammed into the shul.

This serves as the basis for some entertaining Jewish pop culture.

First, because every inch of space is precious, synagogues routinely issue admission tickets to members. The idea is that for these three days (two days of Rosh Hashanah and one day of Yom Kippur), there's just not enough room to welcome non-members. Any other day of the year, of course, all temples are thrilled to include any new faces.

High Holiday tickets are always somewhat controversial. People think (incorrectly) that if you don't pay some exorbitant fee, you can't attend services. The reality is that I've never heard of anyone being turned away from a temple. Synagogues might take your name and other information and hope that you either become a member or make other financial or charitable arrangements after the holidays. Some temples may use the High Holiday season (which often falls near the beginning of the fiscal year) as a way to ensure that members are current on their dues.

But it's hard for spiritual and financial matters to be so intertwined. Jews have been poking fun at the High Holiday ticket situation for generations, and you can often find some reference to it whenever a TV show or sitcom features any Jewish characters attending temple. The best joke that sums up the conflict of "charging" people for synagogue admittance tells of a Jewish guy who approaches the front table in the shul lobby on Rosh Hashanah. "I'm not here for services," he says. "I just need to tell Mr. Goldstein something." The ticket guy behind the desk says, "OK, make it quick. But you're in big trouble if I catch you praying."

The other bit of pop culture is the coining of a well-known term: "The three-day-a-year Jew." This refers to the large number of congregational members who only attend services on the three days of the High Holidays.

I'm not crazy about this phrase. It comes off sounding a bit holier-than-thou, as if to say that people who come to temple on a regular or even occasional basis are more Jewish than those who choose not to, even if they do feel a desire or obligation to come annually. Moreover, those who come only on the High Holidays often use this term to describe themselves in a self-deprecating way, as if to sheepishly apologize for their infrequent attendance.

I say nonsense to both groups. These so-called three-day-a-year Jews may not make much of an appearance throughout the year, but they're involved and engaged enough to belong to a temple in the first place. They're the ones who are on the roster and support the synagogue through their dues and whatever other nonreligious activities they do. I think the biggest mistake any congregational or spiritual leader can make is to cause these people to feel guilty about how often they decide to come to temple.

When a member comes to services on Rosh Hashanah, the last thing he needs to feel is that he's a lousy Jew. (But you *should* be calling your mother more often.)

Sorry About That

One of the most important, most recognizable, and probably most misunderstood themes of Rosh Hashanah is that of *teshuvah*, or repentance. Each year I teach my Hebrew school students about repentance. It only took me about twenty years of looking into blank, glassy-eyed faces to figure out that most kids have no idea what the word "repentance" means. You probably know that it means something like saying you're sorry, but there's so much more involved in the process of repentance.

Rosh Hashanah is supposed to be a time when we examine ourselves and our behavior. We're supposed to acknowledge our faults, figure out where we went wrong, and find ways to improve in the future. Whereas people who like to make New Year's resolutions on January 1 have often forgotten about them by the end of the month, the resolutions and promises that we make to ourselves on Rosh Hashanah are supposed to be more profound and lasting.

Let's look at a concrete example of how a person might start trying to perform the act of *teshuvah*. Imagine that you run a local candy store and I'm a regular customer. One day I go into your store for my usual nougat fix, and as you and I are chatting, your phone rings. You say, "Oh sorry, Cantor [you'd think by now we'd be on a first-name basis], I have to get that. I'll be right back." As you head into the back room to answer the phone, I find myself alone in a store filled with delicious candy. I am overwhelmed by temptation, and I slip my favorite candy bar into my pocket! I then call out to you, "See you later!" and leave the store.

Awful! Thief! How could I do such a thing?

(Disclaimer: This story is a work of fiction. I do not now, nor have I ever shoplifted. If you own a candy store, please let me come in.)

Let's fast-forward a number of months later. It's now time for Rosh Hashanah. We are supposed to take a hard look at ourselves and how we might have sinned in the past year. I suddenly remember that I stole a piece of candy from your candy store, realize that I did something terrible, and want to make things right and begin the process of repentance.

There are a number of possible scenarios that might play out.

Scenario One—Living on a Prayer

I feel awful about what I did. I go to services on Rosh Hashanah, sit through hour after hour of the prayers, read the words in the *Machzor* (the Rosh Hashanah prayer book), and feel that I've reformed. I pray the words asking God for forgiveness and really absorb all the important themes of the day. I leave services after the two days of Rosh Hashanah satisfied that I've taken everything seriously and sincerely, and that the slate is clean for next year.

Someone might listen to that story and come to the logical conclusion that I made it all about me. Meanwhile, you, the candy store owner, are still out some amount of money or inventory because of my actions. That doesn't sound fair.

Let's try again.

Scenario Two—Passing the Buck

I feel awful, same as in our first scenario. But this time, in addition to my fervent and sincere praying on Rosh Hashanah, I realize that I have to make things right with you. So sometime around Rosh Hashanah, I pay another visit to your store. This time, without you knowing, I surreptitiously leave a ten-dollar bill on the counter next to the register. I figure the candy bar itself was only a couple of bucks, so when you find the money later, it will be not only payment for the missing inventory but also a little something extra for the trouble I caused. Even though you won't know who left the money, you'll be paid back for my theft and you'll come out ahead of the game. That's a win-win situation for both of us.

Better? Alas, no. Sure, there was definitely some measure of consequence in this second scenario. I stole something. I paid for it along with an extra amount as punishment. But there's a vital element of repentance that's still missing.

The Jewish tradition teaches something pretty remarkable. In other religions, it may constitute a complete act of contrition to state one's sins and perform some act of penance. In Judaism, though, we must actively seek out the person we harmed or sinned against and ask for that person's forgiveness. All the sitting in temple, praying, and hand wringing in the world have no effect on the wrongdoings that have occurred between two people.

There are sins against God and there are sins against our fellow man. Isn't it ironic that we think nothing of sitting in a temple and praying for forgiveness from God, but we freeze in fear at the thought of going up to a friend, admitting we were wrong, saying we're sorry, and asking for forgiveness? There was nothing particularly challenging about going into a store and leaving a ten-dollar bill on the counter. It was basically taking the easy way out.

Let's try one more scenario and see if we can put this whole sordid candy bar theft to rest already.

Scenario Three—The Apologist

I go into your candy store. I steel my nerve and say to you, "When I was in here the last time, I did something really wrong. I took a candy bar and left without paying. I'm so sorry that I stole from you, I'm ready to pay you back any amount you think is fair, and I promise to never do it again. I hope that you can forgive me."

So far, so good. I've made a nice sincere apology, I've committed to changing my behavior, and I've taken responsibility for the wrong-doing directly with the person who was harmed. Aren't you curious what happens next? Does it have any effect on my act of repentance? Let's see. I imagine this could play out one of two ways.

The first possibility is that you look at me with shock!

"Cantor!" you exclaim. "How could you do such a thing? How could you betray my trust? No! I do not forgive you! Get out of my store right now and never come back!"

Wow, not exactly the happy ending we were hoping for, was it?

Another option is that you respond, "Cantor, I can't believe you would do that, but I appreciate the fact that you told me and that you're paying me back. If you promise to never do such a thing again, then I accept your apology."

That's certainly a happier, touchy-feely ending to the whole story. But it begs this question: If we are to perform the act of repentance by apologizing to those we sinned against, does it matter if the person actually forgives us?

I used a silly example of stealing a candy bar to make things simple and easy to understand. Real life is a lot messier and more complicated. There are family rifts, perhaps caused by one person's hurtful words, which now seem irreparable. Former close friends might never speak again because of overheard gossip. If only all sins were as easy to address as a stolen piece of candy.

We are only able to do the best we can. According to Jewish tradition, we should seek out a person's forgiveness a minimum of three times. Logically, that makes a lot of sense. People who may not be able to forgive right away might change their mind after thinking about things for a while. Coming back again, or even a couple more times, gives the other person a chance to process things and consider the whole matter more rationally.

The Final Step

In performing the act of *teshuvah*, so far we've figured out a couple of difficult but important steps. First, through the act of taking a hard look at your behavior over the past year, you're supposed to see where you went wrong and how you might make some changes. Next, you have to try to make amends.

> What I did wrong—check.
> Apologize and receive forgiveness—double check.
> Good to go until next Rosh Hashanah? Not quite.

We haven't talked about the real, down-and-dirty test of whether a person has really accomplished genuine repentance. Maybe you knew that Rosh Hashanah was coming, got caught up in the meaning of this holy day, and, in a moment of weakness, apologized to everyone in sight. But what about *after* Rosh Hashanah?

The true test of *teshuvah* is seeing whether you've made any real changes. So to continue once again with my candy store example, imagine that it's a number of months later and I find myself once again in your candy store. (I guess you said I could come back—thanks.) And again, your phone rings, you go to answer it, and I am left alone with all those delicious and tempting candy bars. Really, I don't know how you stay in business.

This time is different, though. Sure, I have the same chance to pilfer something, and I'm always in the mood for a snack, but I think back to what I did last time. I remember how it made me feel, and how difficult and humbling it was for me to approach you, admit what I did, and seek your forgiveness. Keeping all that in mind and wanting to feel better this time, I successfully resist the urge.

Behavior—changed. Repentance is complete.

And there's a good reason why we think about *teshuvah* this way.

Remember that one purpose of Rosh Hashanah is making changes. If this holiday were only about seeking forgiveness, that probably wouldn't accomplish the goal. Anyone can look back over the past year and identify times when they've done something wrong or hurtful. Some might go further and apologize. But without that vital last step of promising to change future behavior, a person could easily just figure that whatever he does during the year will eventually be OK once Rosh Hashanah rolls around. In other words, it doesn't really matter what I do wrong during the year, because I'll have the chance to repent each year.

Nice try.

PERFECT FOR FAMILIES

ALL PARENTS teach their kids to say the magic phrases "Please," "Thank you," and "I'm sorry." When a really young child does something to hurt someone else, the parent makes him say that he's sorry, even if that little kid doesn't want to apologize. He's being taught the proper way to behave.

Later, we hope, that becomes learned and routine behavior.

The same goes for performing *teshuvah*. Parents can help their young kids think about things they might have done wrong and how they might change that in the months to come.

All family members might take a turn and identify one thing from the past year that they regret. I think it's very valuable for kids to see that the act of repentance is something that both adults and kids can do.

Shofar So Good

The shofar is one of the most recognizable items in all of Judaism. While it's most commonly associated with Rosh Hashanah, it was used in ancient times on many occasions. Think of it as an early bugle.

Whenever anything really important was to take place in biblical times, a trumpet or horn was sounded. This blast might have served to rally the people to war, or signaled a jubilee year, a time when all debts were forgiven and household slaves were set free.

There weren't too many music stores in the desert, so luckily someone figured out that the horns of certain animals made great instruments. The Torah mandated that this first day of Tishrei (which later on became identified as the New Year) should be marked with the sounding of the horn. It makes no similar pronouncement about any other sacred day. As a result, the shofar—a ram's horn—and Rosh Hashanah are inextricably linked.

Even though the shofar's background is rather prosaic—it was a convenient and common kind of horn—it's much more satisfying to create a reason or rationale for its existence. Therefore, one specific biblical story has become an integral part of Rosh Hashanah, and we read this story from the Torah each year on this holiday.

Abraham and Isaac

Talk about your awkward Thanksgiving family dinners. You think *your* family bickers? At least your father never schlepped you up a mountain to offer you as a burnt sacrifice. Let's look at this story closely. While it remains an iconic narrative, I've always been troubled by some of the details, especially by the supposed moral or lesson that most people are taught.

One day, seemingly for no reason, God decides to test Abraham. "Abraham," God says, "take Isaac, whom you love, up to the mountain and offer him to me as a burnt sacrifice."

How did Abraham respond to this bizarre and possibly cruel request?

Just a few chapters earlier in the Torah, when told that God intended to destroy the evil cities of Sodom and Gomorrah, Abraham tried to talk God out of His decision. Maybe there was a small number of good people in those cities, he reasoned. He enjoined God to let him try finding them. Ultimately, Abraham was unsuccessful, but the notion that even one innocent person would be killed was troubling for him.

Surely now Abraham would protest, bargain, plead. But *without a single word*, Abraham takes Isaac and some servants and sets out for the long journey to their destination. Eventually, when they get to the base of the mountain, Abraham tells his servants to stay back so that only he and Isaac proceed the rest of the way. At one point, Isaac sees that his father has all the fixings for a sacrifice—knife, wood, ropes—and asks, "Where's the animal that we'll be sacrificing?" Abraham famously responds, "God will provide the sacrifice, my son."

After they arrive at the top of the mountain, Abraham takes Isaac and binds him to the altar and lifts up the knife to slaughter him. Just then, an angel appears and stops Abraham. "Don't do it!" the angel says. "Now I know that you truly fear God." Abraham looks up and sees a ram caught in some nearby bushes, and he sacrifices the ram in place of Isaac. Later, the angel goes on to tell Abraham that as a result of his devotion and obedience to God, Abraham and his descendants will be blessed and become numerous. It's because of this ram that we use a shofar on Rosh Hashanah.

But did Abraham truly pass God's test? Does Judaism really sanctify blind and unquestioning obedience? Am I the only one who finds this story abhorrent? There are some compelling hints buried in this story that suggest the lesson is not as straightforward as some Hebrew school teachers might have you think.

Even though this is not the conventional interpretation of this story, I've always believed strongly that Abraham in fact *failed* this test miserably. Remember that Abraham was the original iconoclast—smashing his father's idols to reject the notion that there were any gods but the one true God. Abraham argued and fought God's decree regarding Sodom and Gomorrah. It should have been a simple reaction for Abraham to respond to God's order to sacrifice his son by saying, "No! We do not engage in human sacrifice. The only appropriate sacrifices are animals."

How might we infer that Abraham failed this test? At the crucial moment, just as Abraham was ready to kill his son, it was an angel who stepped in to stop him. Up until this point, God and Abraham communicated directly. Now God sends an intermediary, perhaps because He's angry with Abraham.

In fact, God and Abraham *never speak to each other again* after this story.

Now what about Isaac? I imagine that most people picture Isaac to be a young kid, maybe around twelve years old. It's more likely, however, based on the chronology of the text before this chapter, that Isaac is closer to his mid-twenties. That changes things, doesn't it? Did Isaac, moments away from being slaughtered by his seemingly insane father, simply view this as a harmless test of his father's dedication? What happened when Abraham freed him? Did Isaac just brush himself off, pat his father on the back, and say, "Whew, that was a close one, Pop, wasn't it?"

The text doesn't tell us directly, but there is a very telling sentence. After everything happened, "Abraham returned down the mountain to his servants." Where was Isaac? The text took great pains to tell us twice before that Abraham and Isaac walked together up the mountain. Now, Abraham descends by himself. Is it possible that Isaac broke off all ties with his father after this incident and didn't want to be near him?

In fact, Abraham and Isaac *never speak to each other again.* The next time Isaac sees his father is at Abraham's funeral, with his brother Ishmael.

This story never mentions Sarah, Abraham's wife and Isaac's mother. Was she involved in this at all? Would she have agreed to let her husband commit this act of violence against her son? We certainly imagine that Abraham and Isaac set out on this mission without Sarah's knowledge and consent. The very next chapter following this story begins with Sarah's death. Some commentators have suggested that when Sarah learned where Abraham and Isaac were going, and that her only son was probably already dead at the hand of her husband, she died of shock and sadness.

So now you see why it might be fair to ask if Abraham *really* passed God's test. He no longer communicated with God. He ruined his relationship with his son. His actions may have caused the death of his wife. Abraham arguably destroyed his family and everything that was important to him.

Perhaps we can come away with a powerful lesson for Rosh Hashanah with this interpretation as well. By looking at this story of Isaac's near sacrifice as a cautionary tale, we are reminded very strongly that our actions matter and they can have profound effects on others. We might also learn that blind and fundamentalist adherence to religion without thought or common sense can become dangerous.

Have a Blast

There are three distinct types of sounds that are made with the shofar during Rosh Hashanah.

> *Teki'ah*: One long blast.
> *Shevarim*: Three medium blasts.
> *T'ruah*: Nine very short staccato blasts.

IN DEPTH

THE SHOFAR is not always sounded on Rosh Hashanah. Whenever Rosh Hashanah falls on Saturday, or Shabbat, we don't use the shofar. According to strict Jewish law, it's forbidden to carry items on Shabbat. Just to make sure that no one carries their shofar into the building, we omit that ritual. Because Rosh Hashanah lasts two days, there's always at least one day every year that we hear the shofar. However, those communities that only observe one day of Rosh Hashanah would include the sounding of the shofar regardless of whether the holiday falls on Shabbat.

While there's no single explanation as to where these different types of blasts came from, the different sounds can symbolize distinct moods or emotions to the listener. The long *teki'ah* is like an alert sound designed to get your attention. The three blasts of *shevarim* may be compared to a person's wailing, or crying out for forgiveness. Finally, the staccato notes of the *t'ruah* can function like an alarm clock going off, symbolically serving to wake up the listener and make him take notice.

There's also *teki'ah gedolah*, meaning "really big *teki'ah*," which is pretty much what you think it is. The *teki'ah gedolah* blast is held for somewhat longer than the regular *teki'ah* blast. In most synagogues, this is the time when the shofar blower takes a huge breath and then holds the *teki'ah* as long as he possibly can. Then, when he finally gives up, usually turning purple in the process, the whole congregation chuckles and murmurs approval. I find the spectacle of *teki'ah gedolah* to be a little distracting from the message we're supposed to get from the sound of the shofar. If everyone starts giggling and talking after the shofar blowing, then they're kind of missing the point of what the shofar blasts are supposed to mean to us, aren't they? In fact, the shofar blower is really supposed to hold the *teki'ah gedolah* for a reasonable amount of time, so that it's only somewhat longer than *teki'ah*.

Also, I always wondered what would happen if you had a talented musician up there who was capable of rotary breathing. *Teki'ah gedolah* could go on almost forever.

The Book of Life

One enduring image that we read and learn about every Rosh Hashanah is the so-called Book of Life. While it's an indispensable element of the High Holidays, the theology behind it might be troubling.

Jewish tradition holds that on Rosh Hashanah it is written (and later on Yom Kippur it is sealed) who will live and who will die during the coming year. If that's not dramatic enough, a famous prayer called *Unetaneh Tokef* lists all the ways we might meet our end (by fire, drowning, plague, and more).

To further complicate matters, a very close reading of this prayer makes it unclear whether our good deeds will help to get our names into this book or whether it's a done deal regardless of our actions. That's a pretty scary thought.

A literal understanding of this text implies that everything in the future (or at least for the next year) is already preordained. Isn't that precisely the opposite of what we're trying to accomplish on Rosh Hashanah? Aren't we focused on the fact that we have the ability to choose between positive and negative behavior? If our fates were sealed last September, then what in the world is the point of caring about anything we do during the year?

Therefore, I understand this text not literally but, rather, as a metaphor for the fragility of our lives. Yes, some people will die during the coming year. And throughout the year, when I hear news stories of devastating fires or catastrophic tsunamis, I think back to this paragraph recited during the most recent High Holidays, when we acknowledged that some will die by fire, others by water. Instead of it being a literal accounting of individuals who didn't make the cut for next year, it reminds us that our own time may be short, which is a perfectly appropriate theme of the High Holidays. Don't wait to make positive changes because there may not be as much time as you think. Because of this interpretation, this part of the service can be one of the most dramatic and moving sections of the entire day's liturgy.

Because the Book of Life is an integral facet of Rosh Hashanah, one traditional greeting is *L'shanah Tovah Tikateivu*, meaning, "May you be inscribed [in the Book of Life] for a good year."

Cast Away

Another interesting custom on Rosh Hashanah is called *tashlich*, or casting away. This ritual is performed the afternoon of the first day of Rosh Hashanah (or the second day if the first was Shabbat).

During *tashlich*, we symbolically cast away our sins into some body of flowing water so that we can imagine the sins of the previous year are being carried away. The idea originates with the biblical book of Micah, in which the prophet explains that God will cast off our sins into the depths of the sea. Whether it's the ocean, a stream, or a river, we recite this section from *Micah* and throw crumbs or small pieces of bread into the water. If you don't happen to live near such a body of water, you're allowed to be creative. You might find a small pond or lake. But you don't get extra credit by throwing loaves of bread into the water (unless you've been *really* bad), and this isn't the time to start cleaning out your pantry for Passover.

This is a meaningful ritual for the whole family. Kids love tossing little pieces of bread into the water, and it's a concrete representation of what Rosh Hashanah and repentance are all about. And the fish like it too.

Let's Eat

What would a Jewish holiday be without traditional foods? Rosh Hashanah is no exception.

The challah that we eat during the High Holiday period is round, rather than the usual braided loaf. The symbolism of the round challah is that we view the year, and indeed our lives, as a cycle that goes around and around.

Then we have apples and honey. It's traditional to eat apples—a logical fruit for this time of year because they're in season—dipped in honey. The honey symbolizes the sweetness of the new year to come. We can also dip pieces of the challah in the honey. Want even more honey? Some people will use it to prepare dessert and serve honey cake, another traditional Rosh Hashanah dish. Usually, by the time you're done with dinner and dessert, every inch of tablecloth and all of your dishes will be coated with honey.

On Rosh Hashanah, we wish each other *Shanah Tovah U'metukah*, meaning, "Have a good and sweet new year."

The Bottom Line

Even though the concept of *teshuvah* appears in the Jewish prayer book throughout the year, the rabbis understood that people would be more likely to respond to a special day set aside for just that purpose. Rosh Hashanah is the opportunity to take stock and examine the choices that we've made over the past year. We understand that the goal is not to be perfect; if that were the case, we wouldn't need Rosh Hashanah again in the future. Rather, it's a chance to move closer to Judaism's emphasis on *tikkun olam*, making the world a better place through our actions.

Another vital theme of Rosh Hashanah is that of our own mortality. The imagery of the Book of Life reminds us that we're only able to control our lives to a certain extent. But the liturgy suggests that we can at least stack the deck in our favor through the positive choices that we make.

CHAPTER 2

YOM KIPPUR

NO FOOD FOR *HOW* LONG?

IT'S TRULY amazing that a holiday like Yom Kippur made it past quality control. I can't imagine the sales pitch—"We'll make the Jews sit in temple for the entire day and no one is allowed to eat or drink. It's a sure-fire winner!"

Most Jews associate Yom Kippur with these two aspects of the holiday. There are seemingly endless hours spent in services. Then, of course, there is the requirement to fast for the duration of the day. Even a lot of otherwise nonobservant Jews adhere to this ritual, perhaps because it gives them a feeling of connection to others.

Yom Kippur—literally, "Day of Atonement"—comes on the tenth day after Rosh Hashanah and concludes the period known as "The Ten Days of Repentance." It is considered the most sacred day of the entire Jewish calendar, also referred to by the Torah as the "Sabbath of Sabbaths." Whereas on Rosh Hashanah you begin the process of *teshuvah*, repentance, on Yom Kippur you're supposed to seal the deal. Yom Kippur and Rosh Hashanah make up the *Yamim Noraim*, the Days of Awe, also commonly called the High Holidays.

The Back Story

You would think the Torah would spend at least a chapter or something describing a holiday this important and explaining what you're supposed to do. But we find limited information about Yom Kippur in the Torah, just as we did for Rosh Hashanah. Most of the details came later, provided by the rabbis of the Talmud.

The Torah told us that we should have a sacred day on the first day of the seventh month, Rosh Hashanah. Similarly, the Torah now instructs us to take the tenth day of that same month and make it a "day of atonement." As opposed to Rosh Hashanah, which only got its name later in history, here the Torah does use the words *Yom Hakippurim* (Day of Atonement). We definitely get a sense that the original command in the Torah has a lot to do with how we observe the occasion today. The text directs us to "afflict" our souls on this day, along with the familiar and expected prohibition against doing any kind of work. That last part is pretty much boilerplate for major Torah holidays.

But what does it mean to afflict our souls? Should we sit in a dark room like we're in time-out? Practice self-flagellation? Watch C-Span?

Nope, those are way too easy. The rabbis went for the Jewish jugular and hit us where it really hurt—our stomachs. They interpreted the term "affliction" to mean completely abstaining from any food or drink for the twenty-four-hour duration of Yom Kippur. You want affliction? They sure nailed that one.

Not So Fast

The ritual of fasting seems pretty straightforward at first glance. No eating or drinking. That's it.

However, fasting has taken on a larger-than-life significance for a sizeable segment of the Jewish population. Along with lighting Chanukah candles and attending a Passover seder, this is one of the defining, most universally observed rituals among all Jews regardless of affiliation or level of observance. This is not to say that *every* Jewish person observes Yom Kippur but, rather, that even those who aren't very observant or those who don't even belong to a synagogue are likely to fast for some or all of the day. The result is that the fasting itself has become the central theme of the day.

I have always viewed the ritual of fasting as a dramatic way to achieve the mood and emphasize the importance of Yom Kippur. It's almost as if we're saying that we're simply too busy and distracted to eat or worry about mundane matters like deciding what's for lunch. On Yom Kippur all of our energy should be put into looking back on our actions and deciding how we can change our behavior for the better. That's what repentance and atonement are all about.

Fasting also contains a punitive aspect as well, doesn't it? That would seem to directly follow the Torah's command to afflict our souls. We start with afflicting the body by denying ourselves food and drink, and we assume our minds will follow. On Rosh Hashanah, we talked about making amends and apologizing to people we hurt or sinned against. By fasting all day long on Yom Kippur, we're showing our regret to God for all that we've done wrong and taking a concrete action to show our sincerity. Sure, it's easy to say we're sorry. It's much harder and a lot more convincing when we back it up with a difficult fast.

A lot of people take fasting out of this context and make it the sole objective of Yom Kippur. There are some people who should not fast, and Jewish law absolutely agrees on this point. Those with health problems, pregnant or nursing women, and young kids are among those who not only *shouldn't* fast but are also *prohibited* from fasting. Yet each year there are people, often elderly, who insist on depriving themselves of food and water or who won't take needed medications because they are intent on fasting. Then their bodies spend the next month recovering, or worse.

Similarly, kids sometimes make a game of it, bragging to their friends that they were able to fast or that they made it the longest

PERFECT FOR FAMILIES

I'M NOT suggesting that we make the act of fasting a fun family activity. Only the adults in the household should even be observing this ritual. But there is one way that the entire family can get something out of the practice.

One result of fasting and experiencing hunger is the opportunity to empathize with those who are less fortunate. Even a young person who is not obligated to fast on Yom Kippur might be encouraged to skip dessert or eat a little less than usual for part of the day. It's one thing to have an objective understanding of poverty and the fact that some people don't have enough to eat. It's quite another matter to actually experience what it feels like to go to bed hungry.

Since Yom Kippur is a day when we not only look back on our past actions but also commit to improving ourselves, this is an appropriate time to think about how it might be possible to reach out to others and give more *tzedakah* (charity).

before eating anything. Fasting is only a ritual observed by Jews bar or bat mitzvah age or over. Children younger than thirteen might be encouraged to "practice" fasting by going without dessert or perhaps skipping one meal if practical. Just as we teach kids about prayer and the themes of holidays, we can have them get used to what Yom Kippur should make you feel like. Fasting is an important tool, but it's not the goal of Yom Kippur observance. Rather, it's what helps get us there.

Let's Make a Vow

Along with fasting, there's another ritual on Yom Kippur that has taken on mythic proportions. The Kol Nidrei service is easily among the most identifiable features of the entire holiday. It takes its name from the iconic first prayer that begins with the words *kol nidrei*. I would venture to guess that most Jews have no idea what the actual Kol Nidrei prayer is all about.

The Kol Nidrei service is the very first service recited on Yom Kippur. Because all Jewish holidays begin at sundown, we begin Kol Nidrei in the evening (followed by the morning, afternoon, and concluding services the next day).

The Kol Nidrei text is not a prayer but a type of legal proceeding. The text is not even in Hebrew. We recite Kol Nidrei in Aramaic, the vernacular language spoken by Jews at the time when it was written, just like English is today. For nonreligious subjects, one wouldn't use the holy language of Hebrew; instead, legal and business matters were transacted in the nonsacred language of everyday use at the time, Aramaic.

Furthermore, we do everything we can to create the proper court setting. We have at least two people stand on either side of the cantor or other person leading the service, each holding a Torah scroll, resembling a rabbinic court of three.

So what is this very important legal matter we need to discuss? What could be so vitally important that we begin the most important day of the entire Jewish calendar with its recitation?

In the Kol Nidrei text, we publicly annul any vows that we make between this Yom Kippur and the next. In ancient times, a vow was a sacred, binding thing. People made vows to God and to other people, and these were considered sacrosanct. Because they were so important, when people inevitably failed to live up to a vow they had made, it was considered a dreadful sin. The legal declaration of the Kol Nidrei tries to prevent that from happening. During this time when we are atoning for our sins and seeking to change our behavior, we start things off on the right foot by taking away all opportunity to sin against God by making a vow and then not fulfilling it. Interestingly, the Kol Nidrei text only refers to vows we make to God. This doesn't affect the promises we make to other people.

Another significant facet of Kol Nidrei is the opening sentence that we recite before we get to the legal pronouncement. We declare that in accordance with the court on high (God), and the court on low (that would be us), we give ourselves permission to pray with other sinners.

I've always considered that to be a really fancy way of saying that none of us is perfect. The entire congregation stands together, all of us with our many flaws and acts that we regret. Otherwise, it might look like the cantor and rabbi, along with the others standing with Torah scrolls, are holding themselves as blameless models of behavior, literally standing above the rest of the imperfect public. In reality, everyone is in the same boat. It's a really powerful and compelling statement.

The Kol Nidrei paragraph is considered so important that it's recited three times. This tradition began in order to make sure that every person, even those who came in late, had a chance to hear it.

IN DEPTH

THE MUSIC of Kol Nidrei is perhaps the most recognizable melody of the Jewish year. Many tunes for various prayers can be quite different, depending on what the cantor likes to sing and a congregation's favorite songs. Kol Nidrei, however, is an example of what is sometimes called a *MiSinai* tune—literally, a tune that was given at Mount Sinai. I think it's nice to imagine that before God gave Moses the two tablets on Mount Sinai, he sat Moses down and sang to him a little first. Actually, this only means that there are some melodies that are so old and go back so far they are sung in virtually every Jewish community around the world.

Think about that for a minute. That's pretty amazing.

As Yom Kippur begins, Jews in every location around the world are reciting the same Kol Nidrei text. We take this for granted somewhat because we all use printed prayer books. The words are right there. Worshippers throughout North and South America, Europe, and Australia are all going to find the same words to Kol Nidrei.

But the tune? Up until a few hundred years ago, cantors and musicians didn't notate the music they sang in temple. They passed it along by singing and listening. The distinctive and readily identifiable melody of Kol Nidrei comes to us virtually unchanged through countless generations and, except for a few minor variations, it is sung the same way in Jewish congregations around the world.

So this sets up a little conundrum for us. Because Kol Nidrei is actually a legal, nonreligious piece of business, even recited in the nonsacred language of Aramaic, how can we include this text during what is considered the holiest day of the Jewish calendar? It would be like holding a court session during services. It's not something that would ever normally be done during a holiday.

The answer might surprise you. Traditionally, when we recite Kol Nidrei, it's not actually Yom Kippur. We are supposed to gather in the synagogue and begin this text before sundown, so that Yom Kippur hasn't begun yet. You're not supposed to hold court or engage in a legal session during the actual sacred holiday. Then, as we conclude Kol Nidrei, put the Torah scrolls back in the ark, and end our little makeshift rabbinic court, the sun has gone down, and Yom Kippur has officially begun. And because we've annulled any vows that we might make during the next year, it's a meaningful and positive way to set the tone for the twenty-four hours to follow.

Hurry Up and Fast

So you think you only have to fast for twenty-four hours, right? No problem, you're thinking. I can handle that.

Not so fast with that fast.

You don't get to keep eating and drinking right up until the last minute. It's not like you can stand by your window with a hamburger, watch the sun go down, and just as it makes its last appearance over the horizon, take one more bite, wash it down with a refreshing beverage, and put everything away for exactly twenty-four hours until the next day's sunset.

Nice try.

In fact, what *are* you likely doing at the moment the sun goes down?

That's right—*you're already at temple sitting in services.* I just told you that Kol Nidrei must be recited *before* Yom Kippur actually begins. So your twenty-four-hour fast just got longer by at least another hour or so. In a traditional home, the dinner before Yom Kippur really takes place in the late afternoon.

Like all the Jewish holidays, Yom Kippur's date on the regular calendar will vary from year to year. It can take place anytime between the second week of September and the second week of October. Obviously, this becomes important because the time of sunset changes as well. A year in which Yom Kippur comes early means a later beginning time (later sunset), whereas when Yom Kippur falls in October, sunset comes a lot earlier. In October, a Jewish family might find themselves sitting down for dinner around 4:30 p.m. Everyone has to be done with dinner and ready for services that must begin before sundown.

I should note that this timing is the traditional way to prepare for and recite Kol Nidrei. For a variety of reasons, different synagogues might schedule their Kol Nidrei services for a bit later in the evening, even after sundown. Sometimes temples even have to schedule two Kol Nidrei services back to back in order to accommodate the huge number of people who are likely to attend. They fudge a bit on the Jewish law for logistical purposes.

Keep in mind that now is not the time to try out your new Cinco de Mayo cookbook. Dinner should be . . . well . . . bland. Remember that you're getting ready to go without food and drink for a significant amount of time. It would be a smart idea to avoid eating a lot of spicy or salty dishes that are likely to make you really thirsty.

And what do you do if you're hooked on caffeine, like a good chunk of the population? You probably get ready to have a headache. Some people will make a concerted effort, in the days leading up to Yom Kippur, to taper down their coffee intake in order to make it a little easier to go without. Others just deal with it as best they can.

Remember that the goal of fasting is to add meaning to the sacred day, not to give yourself such a severe headache that you can't even see the words in the prayer book.

The Fasting Back Story: A Whale of a Tale

I bet the average person has a passing familiarity with the story of Jonah. But that's probably limited to knowing that he gets swallowed by a whale and then gets regurgitated after three days. In fact, the story of Jonah has pretty much been relegated to the kids, who love the idea of a cute and cuddly man-eating whale.

The book of Jonah actually deals with some of the most important themes of Yom Kippur. We read the book of Jonah during Yom Kippur afternoon. It is recited as the *haftarah* after the afternoon Torah reading. The *haftarah* is an excerpt from the Prophets, whereas the Torah comprises the first five books of the Bible. You have to imagine that the rabbis placed a huge amount of importance on the story of Jonah to feature this book so prominently on Yom Kippur.

Here's the story.

Jonah was a reluctant prophet. He wasn't so enthusiastic about his role. He was probably more comfortable hanging out at Starbucks and updating his Facebook page. But God appeared to Jonah and assigned him his next mission: There was a city called Nineveh, and all the people who lived there were wicked. God told Jonah to travel to Nineveh to warn everyone that if they didn't shape up and mend their ways, God was going to go all Sodom and Gomorrah on them.

You might remember that Abraham was told something similar back in the book of Genesis. He was upset that such a punishment might be carried out, and he tried to negotiate with God to mitigate such a harsh decree. Jonah's reaction to God's command is quite a bit different. He doesn't seem to be very concerned about the doomed residents of Nineveh, and he doesn't want to have anything to do with this errand. He's more concerned with his own needs and routine, and he doesn't feel inclined to go out of his way for anyone.

Does he tell God no? (Does *anyone* tell God no?)

In fact, Jonah tries to run away. Instead of carrying out God's directions to go to Nineveh, he hops a local ship, perhaps thinking that he might end up in the Bahamas and not have to worry about this prophet business anymore.

But you can't really run away from God, can you? God causes a huge storm to engulf the ship. Jonah and his fellow shipmates are tossed and turned and realize that their ship is about to be lost. The shipmates are paralyzed with fear. It's unclear from the text what Jonah is feeling, but we infer that he knows from the beginning exactly what is going on.

The other shipmates gather to figure out a solution. They discern that there must be some reason for this terrible storm, so they draw lots to see who among them might be the underlying cause. Predictably, Jonah draws the short straw. They ask him, "What awful thing did you do to cause this storm?" Jonah tells them the whole story. He explains that he is a Hebrew, that he reports to God, and that he is fleeing a really important job assignment.

The men on the ship are petrified. They realize how serious this is and that because of Jonah, all of their lives are in danger. Jonah sees this too, and he directs the men to toss him overboard. At first, the men refuse to do so. They don't want to send Jonah to what they assume will be his death. They try to save the ship and row against the wild storm. Only when they realize that their own deaths are imminent do they finally relent and throw Jonah overboard, as he told them to do.

Immediately, the seas calm. The men on the ship are amazed! They realize the power of God and take vows to worship and fear Him from then on. (Notice the "vow" motif again.)

What happens to Jonah after he is thrown overboard? God sends a big fish (not a whale, as universally pictured in pop culture) to swallow him up, and Jonah lives in the fish's belly for three days. That must have been quite a punishment in itself, because Jonah calls out to God from the belly of the fish, prays for his survival, and pledges his faithfulness. Apparently satisfied, God tells the fish to spit Jonah out on dry land.

Jonah, now wet, haggard, and probably pretty smelly, realizes that he can't run from his duty any longer. He travels to Nineveh and, according to God's instructions, warns everyone to change their evil ways or be utterly destroyed.

How do you think the Ninevites react? Do they look at this young, grungy-looking guy and just roll their eyes? No, as it turns out. The king of Nineveh is shocked into action. He decrees that every resident of Nineveh should immediately turn back from their evil ways. He orders a three-day fast, saying that not one person or animal should have any food or water. He tells everyone to dress in sackcloth and sit in ashes. And he includes himself in these actions, stepping off his throne and engaging in these rites of mourning and penitence.

Wow! That was a pretty sincere reaction.

God is pleased with how seriously the Ninevites take the whole thing. He sees that they've turned away from their evil ways and renounced the violence in their hearts. Satisfied, God lifts the decree and declares that the city of Nineveh is spared.

This should be a happy ending, right?

Jonah is the only one not pleased. He throws an adolescent tantrum, saying to God, "See? This is why I didn't want to do this in the first place. I knew you were going to have compassion on the Ninevites and that this whole thing was a big waste of time."

This is a pretty powerful story, and it includes a fair amount of irony. Its themes make it a perfect fit for Yom Kippur. The most striking aspect of the story, of course, is the power of repentance. We learn that everyone is capable of changing their ways and making atonement.

What's interesting in this wonderful story is that everyone Jonah comes in contact with learns this vital lesson except for Jonah himself.

IN DEPTH

JUST LIKE the ancient Ninevites did, on Yom Kippur we practice some of the rituals of mourning as well as fasting.

In addition to going without food or drink, we are also supposed to refrain from any acts of vanity, just as a mourner does. We aren't supposed to bathe or wash. Yes, I know what you're thinking. Not to worry—anything required for hygiene is allowed. The prohibition refers more to making yourself look fancy or to using cosmetic things like perfume.

Because leather was once considered a luxurious comfort, it became traditional to refrain from wearing leather shoes. In temple, you will often see congregants wearing canvas shoes or sneakers. Ironically, these sneakers are often a lot more comfortable than dressy leather shoes. People are also supposed to refrain from sexual relations during Yom Kippur.

All of these actions, along with the more familiar rite of fasting, are intended to demonstrate how seriously we're taking the whole thing.

The guys on the ship, presumably not Jewish, see the power of God, become believers, and vow to fear and worship God. The king and citizens of Nineveh, also non-Hebrews, immediately perform repentance and fear God. Only Jonah, the only Hebrew in the bunch, is not impressed. He is most definitely the anti-hero in this story. Whereas all the other characters in the story immerse themselves in the act of true repentance, Jonah emerges completely unchanged.

The actions of the Ninevites are what inspire our own rituals today. Upon learning of God's decree, they instantly engage in fasting and acts of mourning. The rabbis drew the same connection and mandated that our own repentance and atonement should follow a similar model. Sure, it's simple enough to apologize. But it's much more believable when we back it up with our actions.

I Must Confess

I think that many non-Catholics have a pretty decent familiarity with the ritual of confession. We've seen it portrayed numerous times on TV and in the movies, and we have a pretty good sense of what it's like and its sacred importance within that religion. Did you know that we have confession in Judaism as well? Picture everything you know about the Catholic rite of confession and turn it completely around.

Our version of confession is encompassed in a specific prayer with a very funny-sounding name: *Vidui* (pronounced "vee-doo-ee"). Unlike the customs that most people associate with confession, this prayer is not recited in a closed or private environment (the confessional) to one person (the priest). Rather, the entire congregation stands up together to recite a litany of sins and destructive acts that we as a people, rather than individually, performed throughout the year. The idea is that the entire community must take responsibility in a public setting for their collective actions. It also implies that no one person is any better than anyone else. Instead, we're all guilty of something and need to look back at our behavior and make changes.

The text of the *Vidui* is in alphabetical order, beginning with the first letter of the Hebrew alphabet and concluding with the last. The symbolism here is that rather than try to identify each specific transgression, we show that as humans, we're capable of *all* behavior, from *A* to *Z* (or, in Hebrew, from *aleph* to *taf.*)

Finally, there's no closure to *Vidui*. We don't receive forgiveness after reciting the prayer. There's no redeeming act of penance or particular set of actions that some outside authority orders us to do. The message is that no matter how good we think we are, we still have things that we can improve and ways to make positive changes. We engage in the process of repentance (see chapter 1) and attempt to make amends to others.

Hi, Priest

One of the central themes of Yom Kippur is that of holiness. The day itself is called the "Sabbath of Sabbaths," making it the holiest day on the Jewish calendar. We also read a section from the Torah that deals with the Jewish people attempting to make themselves more holy with the help of the *Kohen Gadol*, the high priest.

Back in the days before rabbis and synagogues, people observed Judaism by bringing sacrifices to the Holy Temple in Jerusalem. The Torah goes to great lengths to describe what kinds of sacrifices and

IN DEPTH

O N YOM KIPPUR, it's traditional to wish one another an "easy fast." I've always thought that didn't make a lot of sense. The entire point of Yom Kippur is to have anything *but* an easy fast. We are specifically told to afflict our souls. Shouldn't we be wishing each other a "difficult fast"?

Apparently other people have also found it hard to reconcile the traditional greeting with the actual meaning of the day, so a new Yom Kippur greeting has emerged in recent years. You might hear people wishing each other a "meaningful fast," which certainly makes more sense.

how many of which animals should be brought for certain occasions and holidays. The high priest was like the CEO of the Temple. He was in charge of making sure that the sacrifices were performed properly, and it was through him that the Jewish people fulfilled their obligations and attained holiness. That was a fairly pressure-laden job.

The Temple was divided into different sections. There was an outer courtyard, and then, as you made your way inside, you would find the altar and the other necessities for preparing and carrying out animal sacrifices. Finally, there was a secret, mysterious area of the Temple that housed the tablets of the covenant (yes, just like in the Indiana Jones movie). This space was entered only by the high priest and only on Yom Kippur.

There is a section of the Yom Kippur service that recalls this moment of utmost power, drama, and holiness. The people would gather around the Temple in fear and awe. The high priest had to make himself ready, both physically and spiritually, for this one transcendent moment of holiness. If he felt that he wouldn't be able to do so, then he had to turn to another of the Temple priests who would take his place. The high priest would enter this closed, secret area, called in Hebrew *Kodesh Hakodashim*, the Holy of Holies, and he would do something amazing.

The high priest would say the name of God out loud.

We have no modern-day parallel. There are numerous names that Jews use to refer to God, the most common being *Adonai* and *Elohim*. But these are just later words that people have come up with. In fact, the true pronunciation of God's name is unknown to us. It is most often represented in Hebrew writing using a tetragrammaton— a four-letter word that is ineffable, not able to be pronounced. When we see this word (יהוה) we just read it as *Adonai*. It helps remind us of the mystery surrounding God and even what we call God.

But back in Temple times, that name, the true name of God that we don't know anymore, held such power and inspired such awe and fear that people were afraid to hear it. On Yom Kippur, when the high priest entered the Holy of Holies, he said out loud that one true name of God. The people made every effort *not* to hear that name! When the high priest uttered that mysterious name, they prostrated themselves on the ground and sought to drown out his voice, proclaiming loudly in unison, "Praised be that glorious name forever!"

YOU'D THINK that the one thing that all Jews could agree on would be what to call God. In fact, it's one of the more divisive issues that exist in Judaism.

The most common word used in prayer for God is *Adonai*. But because that name is traditionally considered appropriate only in the context of prayer, some people will avoid using that word and instead say *Hashem* (literally, "the name") or maybe *Adoshem*, which makes it a little easier to learn and practice the prayers because it sounds similar and has the same number of syllables.

The word *Elohim* is another common way to refer to God. Again, in order to not use God's name in vain, outside of a blessing or prayer, that word might be altered to the similar-sounding *Elokim*. There are other examples of traditionally holy names of God that some people will never use unless they are praying or reading the text of the Torah.

What this leaves out is the fact that these names, *Adonai, Elohim*, and the others, were themselves simple words that people used to avoid saying the *real* name of God, which we don't know anymore. I don't think there's anything inherently disrespectful or unholy about using these terms, even out of the context of prayer, when we're discussing or learning about Jewish subjects.

There is also a more recent trend to use the same strategy not only for the Hebrew names of God but also for the English words. God becomes G-d, and sometimes Lord is written L-rd. Again, there is nothing specifically holy about the word "God." It is just a regular English word, going back to relatively recent European history. It has no basis in Jewish or biblical history and has no religious significance.

In our modern service, we reenact that scene. When the cantor chants the text describing how the people would fall to the ground, he, too, prostrates himself completely in front of the ark. It's an extremely unusual and compelling moment in the service. It's often misunderstood because it relies so much on the ancient and anachronistic imagery of animal sacrifice and the high priest, but this section of the service is really all about the drama. What we modern Jews are trying to do is tap in to that primitive feeling of awe and reverence that our ancestors experienced on Yom Kippur.

Let's Eat, Finally

I've always found it somewhat ironic that many Jews, after having fasted for a full day, will end up eating several days' worth of food in one fifteen-minute sitting. Bagels, tuna, lox, kugel, gefilte fish (always on sale this time of year), juice, coffee, tea, cake, cookies, more cake. Within minutes, no one can remember ever having been hungry.

My advice? Keep it simple. A bagel and a cup of coffee is a great way to break the fast. Your stomach will thank you.

The Bottom Line

Yom Kippur is not a pleasant day; we're supposed to feel a sense of affliction. This holiday gives us the opportunity to devote ourselves completely to the act of seeking forgiveness and making changes in our lives. For one day, we don't worry about basic needs like eating, socializing, or earning a living. Instead, we throw our bodies as well as our minds into the important task at hand.

One vital theme that we see throughout the day is the power of words. What we say matters. We begin by publicly announcing that we should be released from any promises or vows to God that we make during the year. And even the utterance of just one word, the ancient name of God that no one knows anymore, is considered to be of the utmost holiness. Perhaps the act of fasting, refraining from putting anything inside our mouths, is supposed to call attention to the power of what comes out the rest of the year.

CHAPTER 3

SUKKOT

PLEASE STEP INTO THE BOOTH

SUKKOT COMES right on the heels of the very serious Rosh Hashanah and Yom Kippur. We began the Jewish month of Tishrei with the New Year, Rosh Hashanah. Then Yom Kippur fell on the tenth day of Tishrei. If you were hoping for a little break, you came to the wrong month. Just five days later, on the fifteenth day of Tishrei, the festival of Sukkot begins. While Sukkot incorporates some somber themes of survival and God's protection, it also includes some enjoyable and unusual customs.

The word *sukkot* literally means "booths." (*Sukkah* is the singular form of Sukkot.) Sukkot are temporary structures that were built to give shelter, sort of like an ancient version of a tent. One of the most important ways to observe this holiday is to build our own temporary shelter, as we'll see.

The Back Story

Just like its Tishrei predecessors, Sukkot is mentioned in the Torah, and it actually gets a more involved explanation than Rosh Hashanah or Yom Kippur. The text of the Torah tells us that on the fifteenth day of the month of Tishrei we are to observe a festival of tabernacles. That is a fancy biblical way of saying *sukkot*; a tabernacle is simply a booth.

Then things get a little more complicated. We are told that our festival is to last seven days, but we only need to treat the first day as sacred and not do any kind of work that day. We should build *sukkot*, temporary booths, and live in them for the full seven days. This, the text explains, is to remind us that the Israelites built and dwelled in similar temporary structures while they were wandering in the desert.

We are also told to make the eighth day sacred as well. This sounds confusing since the Torah made it clear that Sukkot only lasted seven days. Then what's the deal with this mysterious eighth day? You'll have to stay tuned until the next chapter to find out.

There's also an instruction to take fruit, along with branches of palm and willow, and use them to celebrate the festival. Later on, the rabbis of the Talmud explained very specifically how to incorporate all of these items into our Sukkot observance.

Three's Company

Sukkot, along with Passover and Shavuot (two other important holidays that you'll read about later on in this book), make up what are known as the Three Pilgrimage Festivals. It was traditional for the ancient Jews to make a pilgrimage, a religious journey to Jerusalem, in order to celebrate these holidays. How were they going to celebrate? With animal sacrifices, of course. The Torah lays out in very specific detail what type of animals and how many should be brought to the Temple for sacrifice.

In Hebrew, these pilgrimage festivals are each called a *chag*. Even though you might hear some Jews or Hebrew speakers refer to any holiday—Rosh Hashanah, Chanukah, Purim—as a *chag*, the term only properly refers to one of the Three Pilgrimage Festivals. The word *chag*, related to its Arabic counterpart *hajj*, has the specific connotation of making a pilgrimage within the context of the Jewish calendar.

It's no accident that Sukkot falls on the fifteenth day of Tishrei. The Jewish calendar is lunar (the months follow the cycle of the moon). On the first of any Jewish month, there's a new moon. Therefore, in the middle of the month the moon will be full.

When ancient Jews were making their journeys to Jerusalem and the Temple, there were no streetlights, and they didn't have flashlights to light up the way. So it was pretty convenient to be able to use a bright full moon to make traveling at night easier. Two of the Three Pilgrimage Festivals, Sukkot and Passover, begin when there's a full moon.

We refer to these festivals in Hebrew as the *Shalosh Regalim*. The Hebrew word *shalosh* means "three," and *regel* means "leg," which reminds us that these festivals required the Jews to make their long pilgrimages by foot.

Let's Build on That

What exactly is a *sukkah*? What does it look like and how should we use one to observe this holiday? Simply put, it's a temporary structure with walls and a roof. According to Jewish law, every *sukkah* must have at least two and a half walls. You probably wouldn't want to hire the rabbis of the Talmud to renovate your bathroom. Picture it this way: You could form a *sukkah* in the shape of a big open *U*, and as long as one branch and the bottom of the *U* had full sides, and there was at least half on the other side of the *U*, you were OK. Of course, it's more common to build a four-walled *sukkah* and leave an opening for a door.

The roof of the *sukkah* must be somewhat open to the elements so that you can look up at night and make out the stars. The materials that you lay on top of the *sukkah* to make the roof must be items that grow naturally. You can use branches or pieces of wood (which used to be trees, so that's OK). Many people use bamboo poles. But you can't take a canvas tarp, lay it across the top, and poke some holes in it so you can see the stars. The branches or bamboo or whatever you use to make the roof has a special name: *s'chach*.

The rabbis wanted to ensure that in their enthusiasm to build the best and most durable *sukkah*, people wouldn't use heavy-duty materials. The *sukkah* is meant to be temporary. You can't build something out of concrete and use it every year. It's the opposite of the story of the three little pigs—the least durable and most vulnerable structure is what you're going for.

You are allowed to use different kinds of materials to make up the walls. In fact, some people will construct a *sukkah* that leans against their house, actually making one of its walls the back of the house. That's considered acceptable since the whole structure itself is still temporary. You can use canvas, plastic, or cloth sheeting for the walls—anything that will form a wall and stand up to the elements.

There's no specific size requirement for a *sukkah*. Some are huge, able to fit hundreds of people seated at long tables. You can often find these at major religious institutions that welcome community members to come in and fulfill their obligation to enter a *sukkah*. Other *sukkot* are tiny, with room for only one or two people at a time.

Interestingly, there is no instruction on when the *sukkah* should be built. You would think that the rabbis would have included a timetable for that along with all of the other painstaking details. You might imagine that the construction of the *sukkah* couldn't come more than fifteen days before the start of the holiday, and that on the morning of the day before Sukkot, all building must be complete. But, in fact, there aren't any such rules. That means we get to decide for ourselves how we'd like to proceed.

Sukkot comes just five days after Yom Kippur, which doesn't give you a lot of time to get ready. A nice custom is for people to take the first step in assembling their *sukkah*, even if it's just symbolically placing a piece of wood on the ground, when they get home after the conclusion of Yom Kippur (once they've had their bagel and cup of coffee). This demonstrates their desire and enthusiasm to fulfill the religious obligation of observing Sukkot.

It's traditional, but not required, to decorate one's *sukkah*. Because Sukkot occurs in the fall, many people hang plastic or real fruit from the roof. (Careful—real fruit attracts bees. I learned that the hard way.) Kids are usually happy to string popcorn (one piece for me, one piece for the *sukkah*) or make streamers out of

W HAT IF you'd like to put up a *sukkah* but have never done so before and really have no idea how to proceed? If you're like me, just figuring out what kind of screwdriver to use is a major crisis. Building a complete *sukkah*? Fuhgettaboutit.

Luckily, it's very easy to purchase a pre-fab *sukkah* online or from a brick-and-mortar Judaica store. Some assembly is required, but it's usually a very simple matter of screwing some metal poles together.

Unfortunately, this can sometimes be a fairly pricey option, but the *sukkah* that you purchase will last years, if not decades.

construction paper. Anything to give the *sukkah* a festive and welcoming atmosphere is fine.

Sukkah for Rent

The Torah instructs us to dwell in a *sukkah* for seven days. That's a pretty difficult commandment to fulfill. Are we supposed to move out of our houses and basically go camping for a week? The short answer is yes. That's the intent of the commandment.

There are a few reasons for this. First, the Torah specifically tells us to do it, which is good enough for some people. Second, the Torah explains why—we live in these *sukkot* because our Israelite ancestors did the same thing as they wandered through the desert. Our week-long stay outdoors is intended to remind us of this.

I believe the most compelling purpose of the commandment to live in a *sukkah* is to take us out of our comfort zone. In the chapter about Yom Kippur, I mentioned that one positive result of fasting is to create empathy for, and gain understanding of, those who don't have enough food to eat and who go to bed hungry each night. Similarly, when we remove ourselves from our comfortable, often luxurious homes and spend time in rickety structures vulnerable to the elements, we can much more easily comprehend what it may be like for those living in poverty. Living in a *sukkah* for a short time can be a sobering wake-up call for those of us who take basic living accommodations for granted.

Finally, on a more traditionally religious note, we remind ourselves that while humans might be adept at building strong, permanent structures, everything we have really comes from God. So when we sit in a *sukkah* and hear the wind blowing or feel chilly from the autumn temperature, we realize that our lives are fragile.

What do you do, though, if you're unable to move out of your house for seven days? Maybe it's raining or you live in a climate that makes it impractical to sleep outside during this time of year. What if that's a deal breaker?

Fear not—we have a loophole. The rabbis interpreted the commandment "to dwell" in a way that makes it a little easier for everyone. They interpreted eating a meal to be a form of dwelling. Therefore, even if you're not sleeping outside each night, you should make every effort to eat your meals in the *sukkah*. Furthermore, the Hebrew word used for "dwell" is also the same as "sit." So you can fulfill this important commandment simply by entering the *sukkah*, sitting down, and getting right back up.

Now the real question that's been on your mind since we started: What if you don't have a *sukkah*? Building a *sukkah* is one of the lesser observed rituals. Within a typical synagogue's congregation, a small handful of people might build a *sukkah*, or maybe no one. Most synagogues have a *sukkah* of their own, appropriate for communal use. Usually anyone is welcome to stop by and go in. I have even seen traveling *sukkot*! Sometimes a Jewish outreach organization will put a *sukkah* on the back of a pickup truck (yes, it's allowed—why not?) and bring it to you or to where there might be a large gathering of Jewish people. Have *sukkah*, will travel.

The Back Back Story

I'm picturing a typical *sukkah* that someone might have today. It would properly be topped with branches, bamboo, or some other appropriate material, and you would likely see some nice autumnal

PERFECT FOR FAMILIES

EVERYTHING about building, decorating, and ultimately living in a *sukkah* screams family fun. Well, maybe not the building, especially if you're liable to say a few choice words after hitting your thumb with a hammer. Instead, kids can easily help with the decorations. It's easy to make paper chains out of construction paper, put drawings up on the walls, and hang plastic fruit or other items from the *s'chach* that covers the *sukkah*.

I have also found that kids are often fascinated by the idea of sleeping in a *sukkah*. Perhaps it's because a lot of children like to go camping or sleep in a tent. Whatever the reason, here's a wonderful (and Jewish!) chance to plan a family experience that's a little out of the ordinary. Weather permitting, of course, you might allow appropriately aged children to take a sleeping bag and stay overnight in the *sukkah*. It's also an opportunity for parents and kids to camp out together.

decorations, perhaps some real or fake fruits or other similar items. Its theme would be closer to a Halloween hayride than to something religious.

But is this what the Israelites built in the desert? I can't imagine that they had much access to wood or tree branches. There's not much natural growth going on in the desert. In order to more strictly adhere to the commandment to remember the Israelites' journey through the desert, why wouldn't we be instructed to build a shelter that one would be more likely to find in a desert setting?

To answer that question, let's dust off the time machine that we'll use throughout this book and go back thousands of years. We'll pay a visit to some ancient Canaanites, people who existed long before the Israelites came on the scene. They were pagans—followers of many gods who had no understanding of a monotheistic religion. As we'll see again in the chapter on Chanukah, pagans had no sophisticated comprehension of the world around them. They lived a basic existence of survival, eating what they were able to grow or gather.

Our typical pagan was probably pretty attuned to the climate and the cycle of the year. He would plant his crops, keep a wary eye out for the rain that he hoped was going to come, and eventually harvest and gather his food.

Today, many people keep vegetable gardens. It's fun and satisfying to plant and pick your own food and to be able to serve food that you've grown yourself. Let's say that one year, the local raccoon population decides to have a big party one night. The next morning you look out at your garden and see that most of your prized vegetables are ruined. What a disappointment!

What might you do? Well, you could investigate ways to repel raccoons or other pests in the future. You could examine all your plants closely and see if perhaps a few vegetables could be salvaged. You could wait impatiently for next year to try again, or you could even throw in the trowel and decide that you weren't meant to grow your own vegetables. In any case, what are you going to do now that you don't have a large quantity of fresh vegetables to serve at dinner?

Is this an emergency? Are you going to starve? Of course not. You'll head on down to the supermarket and buy a bunch of produce. Sure, it may be more expensive and a lot less satisfying, but you'll be able to get anything you need, even enough broccoli and Brussels sprouts to make your kids miserable all year.

Not so for our ancient Canaanite friends. Successfully growing enough food was a life-or-death situation. If there wasn't enough rain one year, or some infestation killed a lot of his crops, then a person would not be able to harvest enough food to last all year. He did not have the luxury of a supermarket down the street, and he couldn't depend on any neighbors to help out, because they were likely in the exact same boat. This was life back then—if you didn't have enough food, you starved. Period.

As a result, ancient people took harvesttime very seriously. When it was time to harvest their crops, they dropped everything and devoted all of their time and resources to ensuring a successful outcome.

Imagine that someone might have a really large area of crops to harvest. Envision farm country that spans many miles. Our intrepid farmer wakes up at the crack of dawn on the first morning and works alongside his family harvesting and gathering his crops. By the end of the first day, he's made pretty good progress but he now finds himself a fair distance away from his house.

He could stop work for the day and make the long trip all the way back home. He'd go to sleep, wake up at the same early time the next morning, and have to walk all the way back to where he left off. Similarly, by the end of the next day, and all the subsequent days after that, he'd be farther and farther away from his house, and he'd have to spend a significant amount of time and energy for his "commute" back home. He'd lose hours and hours each day that could better be spent harvesting crops. Remember, if you don't get to the vegetables in a timely fashion, they might rot in the fields and your harvest would be ruined. So this is not just a matter of convenience—time is of the essence.

The farmer has an idea. Wouldn't it make a lot more sense to simply stop for the day and camp out right where he is when the sun sets? Then he'd wake up in the morning and start picking crops again right where he left off. That's brilliant.

He'll need some kind of shelter. Since he can't pick up the phone and order a tent from L.L. Bean, he'll need to be a little creative. He might craft a rudimentary shelter using only the materials that he can find around him. And what would that be? Maybe he's got some cornstalks, branches, and other detritus from his harvest. That should be good enough to make some sort of temporary structure to get him through the night. Then the next day, and each subsequent day, he can fashion the same kind of structure wherever he finds himself late in the day.

Using this kind of efficient time management, the farmer has a much better chance of success bringing in his harvest. In fact, let's go ahead and assume that his harvest is fabulous. He now has enough food to get him through the tough months ahead, and he has all but guaranteed the survival of his family. Nice job.

What's next? Does he plan a celebratory trip to Disney World? (Does Magic Kingdom have a Paganland?) Close, but not exactly. He does, in fact, celebrate with a huge party. If our farmer were a religious man, he might stage a demonstration of thanks to his gods by making a sacrifice—human, not animal. Nothing says thanks for the rain and a good harvest better than offering up a child or two. And all this would take place out in the fields, surrounded by the remnants of the harvest and those booths or shelters that were hastily built each night.

Later in history, the Israelites entered the scene and lived near these indigenous pagans. They, too, began to celebrate their own harvest seasons in the same way as their neighbors. Because this ran counter to the morals and values of their teachings, the rabbis sought to reconcile these harvest celebrations with Jewish meaning. They did so by incorporating a lot of the existing customs into the holiday of Sukkot. This explains why our modern-day Sukkot bears little resemblance to a long sojourn in the desert, as the Torah describes, and has everything to do with ancient harvest festivals.

Do the Wave

The other major commandment on Sukkot is to take four specific types of plants: branches of palm, myrtle, willow, and a special fruit called a citron, which is similar to a lemon. Together, these plants are commonly known as the lulav and the etrog.

The lulav is actually made up of the first three types of plants. First, the lulav itself is a long, stiff palm branch. Attached on either side are the branches of myrtle and willow. They are usually bound together so they comprise one unit. During certain parts of the Sukkot service, we are supposed to hold the lulav and etrog together.

Just as we did when we fulfilled the commandment to sit in a sukkah, we also make a blessing over picking up and holding the lulav and etrog. After reciting the blessing, we then wave or shake the lulav and etrog in six directions—right and left, up and down, front and back—to symbolize that God is all around us.

Later in the service, we form a procession around the sanctuary while carrying the lulav and etrog. For people who have never seen it before, it's definitely an uncommon sight to see a parade of worshippers, each holding a lulav and etrog, walking around the sanctuary.

Where did this strange practice come from? Again, we can look back at pagan rites to get a sense of things. It's certainly not too much of a stretch to look at these unusual items and realize that they resemble fertility symbols. The round etrog is likely a symbol of female fertility, and the tall, pointy lulav . . . well, you get the idea. We shake and wave these items around, and some of the leaves fall off and spread around. If you can't draw the connection between this and pagan images of fertility, then you're just not trying.

I love using the lulav and etrog precisely because they're so unlike anything else we do during the year. Most of the time we spend in services we are sitting or standing in worship, with a certain amount of decorum. Here, we engage in a very primitive ritual. It can be quite jarring, and it really makes you take notice.

There are some other interpretations of the lulav and etrog as well. According to tradition, each of these four species corresponds to one characteristic of humanity. The tall lulav is like a person's spine. The myrtle's leaves resemble the shape of eyes. The willow is like the shape of lips, and the round etrog represents the heart. Because we always use the lulav and etrog together, this symbolizes the different aspects of a person's character functioning as one unit. That's a lot easier to explain to kids than that pagan fertility thing.

Rain on Our Parade

Rosh Hashanah and Yom Kippur, which take place only a week or two before Sukkot, are filled with themes of life and death, deeds and consequence, and judgment and forgiveness. During those sacred days, we get the sense that our lives hang in the balance. Have we successfully performed repentance? Do our actions influence what happens in the coming year? According to Jewish tradition, our fates are written on Rosh Hashanah and sealed on Yom Kippur.

Sukkot continues along these lines. Each day of Sukkot we recite a prayer called *Hoshanot*, from the Hebrew word for salvation. We repeatedly pray *Hoshana*, "Save us!" which is where the Christian exclamation "Hosanna" comes from. What are we hoping to be saved from? Since our fates were presumably decided less than a week before, what kind of danger might we be in?

The theme here is based on Sukkot's harvest and agricultural roots. During the *Hoshanot* prayer, the parade of lulav- and etrog-carrying congregants takes place. We acknowledge that God is the true source of our protection. Like spending time in a rickety *sukkah* all week, reciting *Hoshanot* reinforces our feeling of vulnerability.

What would make us feel more secure? For a harvest-based festival, what would represent the most successful outcome? Rain. Lots of it. In the proper season. We will take a much closer look at praying for rain in the next chapter, but for now, understand that all of this waving of fertility and harvest symbols and parading around are leading us up to the ultimate request for rain. This is how we hope God will save us during the coming year.

Not Wholly Holy

So far, all of the holidays that we've looked at have followed the same format. The Torah has instructions that we are to observe a certain day of the calendar, that the day is to be holy, and that we are to refrain from doing any kind of work.

Sukkot begins the same way. It is a seven-day holiday, but only the first day is observed as a holy day. The rest of the days are referred to as *chol hamoed*, meaning "intermediate days." They are nonsacred days of the holiday. We still observe all the rituals of Sukkot, go into the *sukkah*, and take lulav and etrog, but because the days are not considered holy, we are allowed to do all kinds of work.

There is a difference between how Sukkot (and other holidays) is observed in Israel and the rest of the world. You may remember that when I talked about Rosh Hashanah and the new month in the first chapter, I explained that because the news of when certain dates took place had to travel far distances, sometimes one-day events lasted two days. This was to make sure that people were able to observe the holiday at the proper time even if the information was delayed.

Sukkot follows this pattern, as we'll also see with the other Pilgrimage Festivals. In Israel, where there was never a worry about the distance delaying people getting news, the holiday follows the Torah's directions. The first day is holy, followed by the remaining days of *chol hamoed*. Everywhere else, however, the first *two* days are considered holy, and then we have the remaining five days of *chol hamoed*.

Just like we saw with Rosh Hashanah, most Jewish communities have maintained the two sacred days of the festival outside of Israel even though in modern times we know perfectly well when the fifteenth day of Tishrei occurs.

You Can't Beat This

The last day of Sukkot has a special name. It's called *Hoshanah Raba*. Remember that one of the themes of Sukkot is salvation, and on each day of Sukkot, we recite the prayer called *Hoshanot*. This last day builds on this theme of salvation, to a climactic end.

First, is Hoshanah Raba a sacred day or just another working day of *chol hamoed*? The answer is yes, no, sort of, maybe.

The short answer is that Hoshanah Raba is the last day of *chol hamoed*, so all kinds of work are permitted. But as we'll see, the day itself is an interesting mixture of every kind of holiday.

Let's take a musical detour for a moment and talk about the music of the service. Cantors spend years learning the minutiae of how every word in the prayer book should be sung. Each type of holiday calls for a different kind of *nusach*, which is the set of chanted tunes and melodies that the cantor would use. One kind of *nusach* is used on a regular weekday. The *nusach* is different when chanting the Shabbat service. Then there are different tunes used for various other occasions and holidays, like Rosh Chodesh, Rosh Hashanah, Yom Kippur, Sukkot, and the other Pilgrimage Festivals. In fact, if you took a learned and knowledgeable Jew and randomly plunked him down in a temple on any day of the year, he might be able to figure out the date and even the exact day of the week just by listening closely to the music and the prayers. That's how important the melodies are in temple.

Therefore, you might wonder, how does a cantor sing the service on Hoshanah Raba? Does he or she use a tune for Sukkot? Is it the weekday melody, because it's *chol hamoed*? In fact, it's everything. This is the kitchen sink of the *nusach* world. You have a little bit of everything. Cantors are constantly knocking their collective heads against the synagogue wall trying to keep track of how to lead the service on Hoshanah Raba.

There are elements in this service of the High Holidays, the Pilgrimage Festivals, and plain old regular weekdays. First, the cantor puts on a *kittel*, the white robe used for Yom Kippur, which indicates that maybe this day is a little more serious than you would otherwise think. The liturgy of the service is a mix of those weekdays and holidays.

Just as on every other day of Sukkot, we recite *Hoshanot*, in which we hold the lulav and etrog and form a parade around the sanctuary. But on Hoshanah Raba, it's like having *Hoshanot* on steroids. Instead of performing one revolution around the room, on Hoshanah Raba we make seven circuits.

Why are things ramped up so dramatically? Remember, it's all about the salvation. We've learned that according to Jewish tradition, our fate for the next year is written on Rosh Hashanah. Then, on Yom Kippur, that book is sealed. But on Hoshanah Raba, tradition holds that our sealed fate actually gets delivered to the divine message center. As any airline passenger knows, anything can happen between the time when you send your luggage away and when you hope to claim it at the end of your trip. Presumably, even the message that decrees our fate is not official until the last moment, and that time is Hoshanah Raba.

After the seventh procession around the room, we take the lulav and use it for the first and only time without the etrog. We remove one of the myrtle branches from its binding and whack it three times against a hard surface, such as a table or pew. This causes many or all of the myrtle leaves to come off and scatter to the floor.

There's no escaping the primitive imagery here. As we will see later on when we talk about Chanukah, this is an example of the pagan practice of demonstrating their wishes to their gods. In this case, we are praying to God for two important things—rain and a good crop. The scattering of the leaves symbolically represents the falling of raindrops as well as the spreading of green vegetation. It also gives the custodian a lot to clean up after services.

The Biblical Donald Trump

One feature of each of the Three Pilgrimage Festivals is that we add the reading of a particular book of the Bible to each service.

There are some interesting, lesser-known books that are tucked away in the back of the Bible in the Writings section. On each Pilgrimage Festival—Sukkot, Passover, and Shavuot—we take one book that somehow connects to the theme of the holiday, and we recite that book during the service.

Sukkot's book is a wonderful gem called Ecclesiastes, named after the man who wrote it. If, like everyone else, you have trouble pronouncing that guy's name, you can also use his Hebrew name, *Kohelet*. Much easier. Ecclesiastes is a fascinating character, all the more so because what he says is so *un*-biblical. His statements resonate with us in modern times as if he had been interviewed just last week. So who is he? What does he say, and why do we read about him on Sukkot?

Ecclesiastes was an old, rich guy. He had spent his entire life amassing wealth, real estate, and possessions. He was an ancient version of Donald Trump, but probably with better hair. He had everything, had done everything he ever wanted, and was now in his twilight years. Ecclesiastes looked back on his life and wondered if all of the time spent on accumulating possessions and wealth was really worth all the effort.

He was a realist, sometimes bitter and often cynical. He had no problem with people who, like him, sought to amass a fortune. But he urged people to keep the proper perspective. In the end, he said, it just doesn't matter at all. He observed that most people's motivation to own more and have more money is derived from jealousy of what others have.

Remarkably, and even more significant in light of the themes of the just-passed High Holidays, Ecclesiastes debunks the notion that there's any cosmic system of reward and punishment. He observes that sometimes righteous people die and evil people flourish. There's no rhyme or reason, so stop trying to make sense of it. Just go ahead and live the life you want, because none of it matters in the long run. Everything you do and have and strive for is just vanity and emptiness.

It amazes me that the ancient rabbis took this book and included it in the canon of the Bible. To me, it seems to contradict almost every notion of divine consequence that had been taught until that point. Ecclesiastes does believe in God, but he simply does not hold that there's any rationale to God's decisions about our fates. In other words, don't engage in good deeds or other such acts because you're trying to reap a reward. Do it because it helps create a good life for you right now. Live for the moment.

What connection is there between this book and Sukkot? Ecclesiastes tells us that it's a myth that riches make a person happy. He acknowledges that God, however unpredictable, is ultimately the source of whatever happens to us. This parallels nicely with the insecurity and vulnerability that we feel living outside of our comfortable homes and taking shelter in a flimsy structure.

Let's Eat

With Sukkot, it's less about specific foods, and all about the al fresco dining. While there aren't traditional dishes for Sukkot, we do make the effort to eat in the *sukkah* as often as possible, which lets us fulfill the obligation to "dwell" inside *sukkot*. When Sukkot falls in late October, you might want to include hot soup in your holiday menu, to help you stay warm as you eat outside in the chilly weather.

The Bottom Line

Sukkot is an action-driven, experiential festival. Rather than simply praying words of praise, declaring that God is the true source of protection, we go outside our homes and actually experience that emotion for ourselves. Just as Ecclesiastes did throughout his own life, we spend a lot of our time building things up—our bank accounts, our strong and luxurious homes—only to spend one week living or even just eating outdoors, protected from the elements by only by the most basic structure.

That's one reason why Sukkot comes so soon after the just-concluded High Holidays. It reinforces the focus on the fragility of our lives, and it highlights the idea that no matter how much we try, we can't guarantee our futures.

CHAPTER 4

SHEMINI ATZERET
AND SIMCHAT TORAH

THE HOLIDAY THAT
NO ONE KNOWS

S A not-so-famous Jewish comic (OK, my son) once
quipped, Shemini Atzeret is the perfect Jewish holiday. You
can use it as an excuse to get out of anything with non-Jewish
teachers and bosses because it sounds authentic and important. And
since no one has ever heard of it, they don't know when it takes place.

The day after Shemini Atzeret is called Simchat Torah, which is
undoubtedly more familiar to some people. In fact, these two holidays, which couldn't be more different in theme and emotion, are
actually two sides of the same day. Only later in Jewish history did
they get separated into consecutive days, and even that depends on

the specific Jewish community and how they observe the calendar. Let's first talk about Shemini Atzeret, and then we can discuss its alter ego, Simchat Torah.

It turns out that Shemini Atzeret really is an important day. Depending on how you look at it, it's either the eighth and last day of Sukkot or a stand-alone festival of its own. In fact, I had to make a choice when writing this book. Should I include Shemini Atzeret and Simchat Torah within the chapter on Sukkot, or do they each get their own chapter? I considered calling this chapter 3½. One hint that suggests Shemini Atzeret and Simchat Torah are a stand-alone festival is that while we are permitted to still eat our meals and spend time in the *sukkah*, we are not obligated to do so, and we wouldn't make a blessing over the ritual as we did on Sukkot.

A lot of Jews are unfamiliar with Shemini Atzeret, which is filled with sacred meaning, because it gets overshadowed by the flashier festival of Sukkot, with its well-known rituals and customs. Simchat Torah, however, is a lot more familiar, especially to families with younger children.

The Back Story

I hope you remember from the previous chapter on Sukkot that we read in the Torah that the fifteenth of the month was a sacred day that begins a seven-day festival in which we were instructed to dwell in *sukkot*. The Torah then told us that we should make the eighth day holy as well. That might have caused a bit of confusion because according to the Torah, the festival of Sukkot only lasts seven days. What is this mysterious eighth day that we read about?

Shemini Atzeret—literally, "the eighth day of assembly"—serves as a distinct and holy day. It represents the end of Sukkot but has some serious themes of its own. The word *atzeret*, meaning "assembly," is also derived from the Hebrew root meaning "to stop." It's as if the Torah is talking to those worshippers who made the pilgrimage to Jerusalem for Sukkot. Now they're ready to return home, and the Torah says, "Stop! Don't go just yet. We were having such a nice time together. Stay another day."

Make It Two Days

By now, you're getting to be something of an expert on the Jewish calendar, and you may already have figured out this next part. Remember that most one-day holidays become two-day occasions outside of Israel. So Shemini Atzeret, the festival on the eighth day after Sukkot, is celebrated for two days. But rather than observe Shemini Atzeret for an identical second day, we go off-script and celebrate a remarkable holiday in its own right: Simchat Torah—literally, "rejoicing with the Torah."

There's no biblical mandate for Simchat Torah, which is a little ironic since the holiday exists to honor and celebrate the Torah. If we were to stick to the program for all of the other one-day festivals that are celebrated for two days outside Israel, we would simply duplicate our observance for a second day. But Shemini Atzeret and Simchat Torah could not be more different from each other. It's almost as if the rabbis are telling us, "You've all been working and praying so hard for the past three weeks. Now it's time to let loose a little."

Simchat Torah comes as a cathartic release after spending so much time on matters of life and death. On this holiday, we mark the end of the Torah reading cycle by reading the very last portion of text, and then immediately going back to the beginning, the book of Genesis, and starting over.

But first, we need to get through Shemini Atzeret.

More Rain?

It seems like all we've been doing lately has been talking about rain. On Sukkot we started thinking about the harvest and our need for rain. We marched around the sanctuary holding the lulav and etrog and praying for salvation, which really referred to the proper amount of rain. Why is there such an emphasis on rain? Do we live in a desert or something? Would it be so awful to pray for a nice beach day for a change?

Blame it on the farmers. While we're all hoping for some beautiful autumn weather, they're watching their crops closely and keeping a wary eye on the sky. They know that if they don't get the proper amount of rain when they need it, the crops are going to suffer.

While that might mean higher food prices for us living in modern times, it would have been disastrous for our ancestors. There's a reason a lot of the reward-and-punishment language in the Torah is framed around rain. In the second paragraph of the *Shema*, one of the best-known Jewish statements of faith, we read that if we observe God's commandments properly, God will reward us with rain in the proper season (as opposed to a year's worth in one very soggy afternoon), our crops will grow, and we'll have all the food we want. If we disobey God, however . . . well, don't go there. God will withhold the rain, we'll have no food, and that'll be the end of that.

Therefore, rain is emblematic of life and sustenance. Everything that we strive for is derived from that. On Shemini Atzeret, we continue the theme that we started on the recent High Holidays and then on Sukkot, and hope that we are being judged favorably by God. But this time, that judgment centers around rain. We recite *Tefillat Geshem*, the Prayer for Rain, as part of the service. This is a big deal. We don't just add a special paragraph buried within the service. Instead, we make a pretty major production out of it.

Every Shabbat and holiday service traditionally includes a *Musaf* service—literally, an additional service. In most cases, it's not too long and its themes center around the historical existence of the Holy Temple and the sacrifices that used to be brought in those times. Because it does hearken back to an ancient subject, some prayer books, particularly in Reform synagogues, might omit this service altogether.

On Shemini Atzeret, the *Musaf* service is dominated by the Prayer for Rain. The cantor puts on his white robe, the *kittel*, as he did on Yom Kippur. This reminds everyone that we mean business here (and that unsuspecting congregants will have to wait a bit longer for lunch).

If you had to write your own prayer for rain, expressing your desire and need for rain, I wonder what you would say. What strategies would you include in your text to persuade God to send rain? I imagine that a lot of people might list the benefits of rain and how much we depend on God to send the right amount when we need it.

The author of *Tefillat Geshem* uses a pretty clever strategy: good old-fashioned Jewish guilt. Instead of just asking for rain because we need it to survive, the author brings up all the times throughout history that God provided water and rain for our biblical ancestors. In other words, *they* got the rain they needed. You did it for *them*—what, we aren't good enough? We invoke our patriarch Abraham and metaphorically connect his devotion to God with trees and plants sustained by water. Then we pray, "For Abraham's sake, send us water!"

The prayer continues with other major characters like Isaac, Jacob, and Moses, who was saved by the waters of the Nile as he floated to safety. Don't do it for us, God, do it for *their* sake. I've always found that to be a pretty compelling way to ask for something important.

Rain Delay

Why is this occasion the first we're really praying for rain? To be sure, we've had rain on our minds before this day. On Rosh Hashanah, we engage in the act of *teshuvah*, repentance. We concern ourselves with examining our character and our deeds, and how to best make amends. On Yom Kippur, we deprive ourselves of food and water in order to "afflict our souls" and bring a level of seriousness and dedication to our prayers. During the course of both of these High Holidays, the specter of life and death hangs over us. In the climactic prayer recited on both days, we read that God's fate for us will be written down on Rosh Hashanah and then sealed for good on Yom Kippur (and finally delivered to the cosmic warehouse on Hoshanah Raba—see chapter 3). The text that we read lists all the ways that humankind can meet its end: plague, earthquake, famine, fire, and other unsavory events. Then on Sukkot, we think nonstop about the harvest and its utmost importance to our ancestors' survival, all based on rain.

But I wonder why rain is not more prominently featured on those holidays. After all, rain *is* life. And we need the right amount of rain during the proper seasons. If we're so concerned with our survival, why have we delayed actually asking for rain until after the High Holidays are over, and then even longer while we get through all of Sukkot? It's only on Shemini Atzeret, about twenty-two days after the New Year has begun, that the cantor puts his we-mean-business *kittel* on and prays for the one thing without which nothing else matters.

WHENEVER they pull out the fancy music, you know it must be a fairly important occasion. Let's set the scene: we're getting ready to begin the *Musaf* service, the cantor walks out on the bimah wearing his white Yom Kippur finery, and everyone is preparing to pray for the most basic, life-sustaining substance there is. Do you think the cantor just mumbles his way through the prayer?

In fact, the Prayer for Rain is so important that it gets its own special melody. There is a distinct mode—a set of musical tunes and motifs—that is used only for this one prayer and the parallel Prayer for Dew, which is recited on Passover. In fact, a discerning and musically knowledgeable worshipper would find similarities between this melody and the one used only for the concluding service of Yom Kippur.

The music further helps tie together all of our important themes—judgment, life and death, survival, and rain.

This is a spiritually challenging question with a rather prosaic answer, I'm afraid. The rabbis felt that it would be inappropriate to ask for the rain to begin when everyone would be preparing to celebrate Sukkot. Remember that throngs of pilgrims would be making their way to Jerusalem at this time. Then everyone was commanded to dwell in their *sukkot* for the seven-day duration of the festival, something that would be difficult or impossible to do if it were pouring the whole time. It would be much better, they figured, to delay our recitation of the Prayer for Rain until the conclusion of Sukkot. I guess they were pretty confident that their prayers would be answered immediately.

In Memoriam

On Shemini Atzeret, we recite another short service called *Yizkor*, the memorial service for departed relatives. *Yizkor* is included in the service just four days each year—the concluding day of each of the Three Festivals (which is another hint to us that Shemini Atzeret is really the last day of Sukkot) and Yom Kippur.

Stripped down to its bare bones, *Yizkor* is not much of a service. We read brief paragraphs of text remembering specific immediate family members who have died, as well as the traditional memorial prayer for all departed. Then the Mourners' Kaddish, a prayer recited by individuals after someone has died, is read.

However, like other prayers that have modest beginnings, *Yizkor* has become somewhat larger than life. It has been transformed into an important occasion, even for those congregants who are not likely to attend services throughout the rest of the year. Any regular synagogue attendee knows that on the days when *Yizkor* is recited, a larger-than-normal crowd is likely. Many congregants feel that participating in the *Yizkor* service in memory of their relatives is a fitting and meaningful way to honor their memories, and so they make a concerted effort to attend when they otherwise might not. As a result, the *Yizkor* service will often be expanded to include additional readings in Hebrew or English, more prayers, and perhaps a short sermon or other introduction from the rabbi.

Another interesting custom that has become increasingly popular is to have all children who are in services leave the sanctuary during the recitation of *Yizkor*. There are a few different reasons this might be done. One reason is out of decorum; in order to maintain a somber and respectful atmosphere during *Yizkor*, it might be a good idea to take out any young children who might prove to be a distraction. It's hard to create the proper mood when little kids are making noise. The second reason would be one of sensitivity. During the *Yizkor* service, it's typical for many worshippers to remember a parent who has died. Having young children present, presumably with both of their parents still alive, might make someone feel even worse about their own loss.

Finally, another reason why it's the custom in some shuls for all the children to leave during *Yizkor* may surprise you. It has to do with a superstition that the presence of children may be considered too tempting for the angel of death, almost as if one were tempting fate. There's a Yiddish term for this, *keynahara*—literally, "the evil eye." I find this rationale less than compelling. I don't see any need to remove children from the sanctuary during *Yizkor*, provided that they can remain well-behaved and respectful (like they would be during the rest of the service anyway). It's important for children to learn how the Jewish tradition deals with all aspects of people's lives. Still, if you're asked to take the children out, or you think you're getting dirty looks from people around you, it's always nice to follow whatever is customary in that particular synagogue. When in Rome, and all that.

Finally, a Time to Rejoice

Simchat Torah comes right after Shemini Atzeret, and its mood is completely the opposite of what we've been dealing with. Whereas Shemini Atzeret was laden with heavy themes of life and death, praying for rain, and remembering our departed family, Simchat Torah is an occasion when we're encouraged to let loose and have some fun in shul.

It's interesting to note that Simchat Torah, relatively speaking, is a more recent addition to the Jewish calendar as the second day of Shemini Atzeret. The name of the holiday doesn't appear until centuries after the biblical period, and it wasn't really until about the fifteenth century or so that the idea of celebrating the completion of the Torah reading cycle became popular throughout the Jewish world. Prior to that, this day was, in fact, simply observed as the identical second day of Shemini Atzeret.

Everybody Dance Now

On Simchat Torah we recognize completing the cycle of Torah reading and beginning again. While that sounds pretty simple, we make a big deal about it. Essentially, it's like we're all throwing a big party for the Torah scrolls. A lot of the action takes place during the evening service for Simchat Torah. Remember that just that same morning, everyone was still in a serious state of mind for Shemini Atzeret. Then that Jewish day ended at sunset and Simchat Torah took over.

The evening service for Simchat Torah is unusual in that it centers around the taking out and reading of the Torah, something that's not traditionally done at any other evening service. Additionally, while temples may own numerous Torah scrolls and house them in the ark, typically only one or two are used regularly. On Simchat Torah, though, all the scrolls are taken out of the ark and carried around the congregation. Because it's considered a special honor to carry the Torah, as many people as possible make an effort to take a turn holding the Torah and participating.

The Torah service features special processions around the sanctuary called *hakafot*. Back in chapter 3 we learned about a special part of the service for Sukkot called *Hoshanot*. During *Hoshanot*, we marched around the sanctuary holding the lulav and etrog, praying for salvation. It was dramatic and served as a perfect continuation of all those High Holiday themes.

Now Simchat Torah comes along and turns *Hoshanot* on its head. Again, we make processions around the sanctuary, but this time they will be filled with song and dancing. And we make seven revolutions around the sanctuary, just like on the last regular day of Sukkot, called Hoshanah Raba. That's no accident—it's supposed to be an unmistakable parallel to that holiday.

Some synagogues really pull out the stops for Simchat Torah. Services at large urban temples can become singles events, a perfect venue for available Jewish people to meet, dance with the Torahs (and each other), and celebrate. Often temples will get permission to block off the adjacent streets so that the revelry can spill outside the building. In temples that allow musical instruments on Jewish holidays, there might be a small band or *klezmer* group playing as well. Clearly, the contrast between this holiday and Shemini Atzeret couldn't be more striking.

Once you've completed the seven *hakafot* and all the dancing and singing are over, then what? Do you just put the Torah scrolls back in the ark and say, "See you next year!"? Not quite. Even though we do not otherwise read Torah in any evening service, it would be considered disrespectful to the Torah to take it out of the ark and not read from it. So on this one occasion, we insert a brief Torah reading into the evening service. Surprisingly, there's no specific requirement on exactly what you have to read. Most congregations will chant some verses from the last *parsha*, or weekly reading from the Torah (but not the last words—that is saved for the morning service). Others will choose one of the Torah scrolls that people have been using for dancing and singing, open it up, and read a random passage.

Good Morning

The Torah scrolls take center stage during the morning Simchat Torah services as well. All the scrolls are taken out of the ark and, just like at the evening service, we have seven *hakafot* filled with dancing and singing. This time, though, we read more than just a token couple of paragraphs of text out of the scroll. At this service, it's customary to give everyone present an *aliyah* (plural, *aliyot*; the honor of being called to read from the Torah). On a run-of-the-mill weekday when we read Torah, three people are called up to the bimah for *aliyot*. If it's *Rosh Chodesh*, the new month, then there are four. On Rosh Hashanah and the Three Pilgrimage Festivals, we have five *aliyot*, and on Yom Kippur, six. And finally, on every Shabbat, there are seven *aliyot*.

If everyone gets an *aliyah* on Simchat Torah, what if two hundred people show up for services? We'll be there for days! Not to worry—Jews wouldn't do anything that would delay lunch that long. It's customary to call people up in groups to have their *aliyah*. Some bigger shuls might even have two concurrent Torah readings going on from different podiums.

Another fun and interesting tradition on Simchat Torah is for all the children to get an *aliyah*, something that is not done on other days of the year because normally a person must be of bar or bat mitzvah age (thirteen) to receive an *aliyah*. But on Simchat Torah, when we intentionally have some fun with the rituals, we call up every child en masse and an adult will lead them in the *aliyah* blessings.

Finally, there are two significant additions to the Torah service that are only done on Simchat Torah. We formally end the reading of the Torah, and we give that *aliyah* to an honored member of the congregation. After the last word is read, we take another Torah scroll, already set to the proper place, and begin reading from the very beginning of Genesis. The Torah reading goes through each of the seven days of creation.

The symbolism is striking: as Jews, we never consider ourselves done with Torah study. Unlike other texts that we might study throughout our lives, we don't come to the end of this one and declare that we're finished. Instead, we go right back to the beginning without a pause and start reading it again, continuously throughout our lives, to show that the act of learning and studying Torah is something that is never completed.

More Fun

Because Simchat Torah is a day when we're supposed to have some fun, some silly customs involving the Torah have become popular during services. The first centers around *hagbah*, the act of lifting the Torah from the podium at the conclusion of the Torah reading. Usually, a person grasps the two wooden handles of the Torah and, using the edge of the table as a fulcrum, pushes down and then lifts the open Torah straight up in the air. Since the Torah text will be facing away from the congregation, the person turns around in place so that the congregation will get an opportunity to see the inside of the Torah. Then he sits down and the Torah is dressed with its binder and cover.

On Simchat Torah, the person called for *hagbah* sometimes does it differently. He might cross his hands—holding the left handle with his right hand, and the right handle with his left hand—and then lift the Torah up. Next, in a fluid motion, he straightens out his hands and . . . ta da! The Torah text is now facing the congregation. It's a bit of an awkward maneuver, but it's fun to watch. What makes this a bit dicey is that the Torah is unbalanced. Because we are reading from the very end of the Torah, all of the parchment will be wrapped around the handle on the right, with very little weight on the left. That makes lifting the scroll in a normal manner tricky enough, but reversing your hands puts all the weight on your left hand (usually the weaker one). The moral of the story: Don't try this if you're a *hagbah* beginner, or lunch might be delayed longer than you think.

Another Torah-related activity that has taken on increased popularity in recent years is completely unrolling the Torah for people to see. Think about that for a minute. Each week we take the scroll and roll it forward just a little as we read that week's Torah portion. How would the Torah look if we *completely* unrolled it?

Long. You're gonna need a bigger table.

In fact, you really need a large room. The best way to do this is to form a huge circle of standing participants. While being held upright, the Torah is slowly unfurled while each person gently holds the very top of the parchment, being careful not to touch inside. Eventually, the Torah makes its way around the entire circle while many people are holding it up. Obviously, you have to make sure there are enough people who can do this, and also ensure that there aren't a lot of kids running around. Another method is to line up a series of long tables and lay the unrolled Torah out flat. The problem is that you need a *lot* of distance to do that. Even if you had enough tables, it would be difficult to find the space to line them up end to end, since the average Torah scroll is almost 150 feet long.

Once the Torah is completely open, it's fun for the rabbi or cantor to "walk" everyone through the whole thing, pointing out significant passages like the Shema or the Ten Commandments and other unusual features of the text. Kids and adults can also try to find portions of the text that they recognize.

Doing the Opposite

If I had to characterize the nature of Simchat Torah in one term, it would be the "anti-service." Most of the distinct customs that we have on Simchat Torah are the exact opposite of anything we'd expect in temple the rest of the year. Many go against the usual *halachah*, the Jewish law of how we're supposed to conduct services. Let's review some of these customs and see why they're so different.

First, it's usually against the rules to have group *aliyot*. Sure, in modern shuls you might bend this rule a bit, such as calling up a married couple invited to a bar mitzvah service. But traditionally, you're supposed to honor one person at a time. On Simchat Torah, that rule goes out the stained-glass window, and we call up large groups for collective *aliyot*.

Next, you probably know that getting called up for an *aliyah* is something reserved for adults—in Jewish tradition that means anyone thirteen years of age or older. Indeed, the whole point of the bar or bat mitzvah service is to mark that important occasion when a child becomes eligible to receive an *aliyah* and take on other responsibilities in the Jewish religion. But on this holiday, all kids are invited up to have an *aliyah*.

We haven't discarded every shred of tradition here. The group of children should be accompanied by at least one adult so that the blessings over the Torah that are recited will be "kosher." According to this reasoning, it's really the adult who is getting the *aliyah* and he just happens to be schlepping up a hoard of kids with him.

As noted before, we never read the Torah at night. I'm sure this comes from ancient times when there wasn't electricity. Reading Torah in public was something reserved for the daylight hours, and therefore on every single occasion when the Torah is read in shul, it's done during either the morning or the afternoon services. But Simchat Torah flips that law upside down. On this one holiday, we take the Torahs out, conduct a Torah service, and read from the scroll during the evening.

We also take a polite jab at the *halachah* by unrolling the Torah all the way out. According to tradition, you're not really supposed to expose more than about three columns of text from an open Torah, out of a sense of respect and modesty for the Torah. This instruction is routinely ignored throughout the year. The person performing *hagbah* might be feeling extra confident, and so will open the Torah *way* up, as wide as his arms will go, and lift the Torah, showing off not only his superior strength but also about ten or more columns of text. You're not supposed to do that, but who's going to tell him and make Mr. Muscles upset? Normally three columns is plenty, but on Simchat Torah? Open that Torah up the entire way and show it off to everyone.

The seven *hakafot* that we include in the Torah service are in direct opposition to the seven *hoshanot* of Hoshanah Raba. During that holiday, someone opens the ark, takes one Torah out, and stands on the bimah while everyone marches around the sanctuary. On Simchat Torah, we take *all* the Torahs out and use *them* for the procession. One is a solemn and serious occasion, and the other is filled with dancing and singing. It's almost as if we are politely making fun of how serious we were just a couple days before. The rabbis wanted to emphasize the atmosphere of exuberance and joy over completing the reading of the Torah. It's a little like a teacher giving her students permission to bring in food to class and watch a movie at the end of the school year. It's allowing something that's usually not done in a certain circumstance in order to lend an air of celebration for a job well done.

Finally, any suggestion of decorum is gone. Not only do we usually include a lot of kids (and, therefore, noise) in the service on Simchat Torah, but we actually go out of our way to be silly. Some congregants will toss candy or sweets at the guy leading the service or reading the Torah (try doing that on Rosh Hashanah). Others will play little practical jokes like tying the *tzitzit*, the fringes, of someone's *tallit* (prayer shawl) together. *Don't* try this with shoelaces, though, or "Rejoicing with the Torah" is going to become "Explaining why the cantor is lying there with the Torah and a sprained ankle."

Same-Day Service

A little while ago, I reminded you about the peculiarities of Jewish holiday observances outside of the land of Israel, in which some one-day holidays are celebrated for two days. Shemini Atzeret lasts two days, with the second day having been transformed into Simchat Torah. What happens, though, if you're celebrating in Israel? If you only observe Shemini Atzeret for its original one-day duration, as mandated in the Torah, what do you do with Simchat Torah?

In fact, in Israel, and also in some Reform congregations in this country where only the original one day is observed, both Shemini Atzeret and Simchat Torah are combined. You include all the customs and rituals associated with both days. That makes for one long and confusing holiday. You have the vital prayer for rain and the solemn *Yizkor* service juxtaposed with the fun and excitement of dancing with the Torahs and making seven *hakafot* around the sanctuary. Since each holiday has its own distinct mood, I've never understood how worshippers in this situation can attain the proper state of mind.

Let's Eat

Even a traditional food on Simchat Torah pokes fun at another holiday. On Simchat Torah, it's customary to eat apples. Since your kids aren't hyped up enough from a couple hours of dancing, singing, and horsing around, some shuls will serve candied apples or apples dipped in chocolate. This, of course, reminds us of the apples dipped in honey that we traditionally eat on Rosh Hashanah. It's really the perfect parallel. Rosh Hashanah was the first of all these holidays, and Simchat Torah is the last. How appropriate that we eat the same traditional food for both.

The Bottom Line

Shemini Atzeret and Simchat Torah are like twin siblings that look nothing alike. They are both derived from the same day—the mandated eighth day after Sukkot as described in the Bible. Because most Jewish holidays are celebrated for an extra day outside of Israel, this one solemn day became two days, with the more recent second one transformed into a day of utmost celebration and joy.

Shemini Atzeret itself is really the culmination of Sukkot, with many of the same themes. We concentrate on the need for rain, since we've been thinking nonstop about the harvest, and we stress the idea that our survival really depends on God, just like we thought about when we spent time in *sukkot*, outside of our secure homes and exposed to the elements.

Finally, Simchat Torah is the exclamation point at the end of the entire High Holiday season. Just as Rosh Hashanah and Yom Kippur forced us to look at ourselves and make a fresh start, we do the same with our acceptance of the Torah and willingness to keep reading and learning for another year.

CHAPTER 5

CHANUKAH

IT'S A MIRACLE
ANYONE CAN SPELL IT

C HANUKAH may well be the most recognized and universally observed Jewish holiday in modern times. Along with fasting on Yom Kippur and attending a seder on Passover, lighting Chanukah candles makes up what I like to call the Holy Triumvirate of Jewish Observance. It almost seems unnecessary to include a chapter on this holiday since you probably think you know all about this festival. Menorah—check. Miracle of the oil—check. Dreidl—check.

Not so fast. There's more here than a bunch of latkes and chocolate coins.

Does It Pass the Spell Test?

We've all seen the myriad, tortured spellings:

> Hanukkah
> Hannukkah
> Hanuka
> Channukah
> Channukka
> Hanukka

And how do you pronounce it? With an *H* or that fun, guttural *chhhh* sound? How do we try to begin to understand all about this holiday if we can't even agree on how to spell it or pronounce the name?

The name of this holiday is a Hebrew word that means "dedication." Later on we'll figure out why it's called that and why most people don't know the real translation of the word. Because it's a Hebrew word that we simply transliterate into English, the fact is we don't have one official spelling. All we're doing is sounding out the Hebrew word using English letters.

I've never fully understood why the *H* sound and spelling have become so popular and accepted when the Hebrew word starts with the letter *chet*, which uses the guttural *chhhh* sound. Even if some people have trouble pronouncing it, we should at least spell it so that it resembles the original Hebrew word. Therefore, I prefer to spell our holiday "Chanukah" because that most faithfully corresponds to the Hebrew term. I bet by the end of this chapter you'll get really good at making that throat-clearing sound.

The Back Story

Yawn. Here we go again. Another tired retelling of the most well-known Jewish tale of all times.

Maybe. Then again, maybe not. Bear with me and let me know if this story sounds familiar.

Our scene is Jerusalem and the ancient Land of Israel, which throughout history has been fought over and controlled by various empires. If you take a good look at a map, you can easily see that this one small region represents a vital crossroads linking Asia, Europe, and Africa. No wonder it has been the scene of fighting and strife for so many years.

A couple thousand years ago, the Greeks, led by King Antiochus, were the latest superpower to control Jerusalem. Perhaps Antiochus's distaste for the Jewish people can be traced back to first grade, when little Menachem Goldfarb called him "Auntie Tuchus"—we'll never really know. Whereas previous rulers had successfully tolerated the Jews and their distinctive rituals and traditions, Antiochus instituted a policy of Hellenization. From now on, the law dictated, all citizens were required to conform to Greek culture and ideals and they were not allowed to practice their own religion.

What were some of the hallmarks of the Hellenistic culture? First, Greeks worshipped the human body, considering it a thing of art and beauty. They wore skimpy robes, hung out in the gym, and spent a lot of time engaged in public athletic competitions. Next, they not only didn't practice circumcision but also outlawed it completely. If the human body is a piece of art, they reasoned, then you don't change any part of it. Circumcision would be considered a desecration, altering a form of perfection. Additionally, Greeks worshipped idols and built statues and other monuments to their gods.

The ideals of Greek culture ran counter to the observance of Judaism. Jews, never a formidable presence in sports to begin with, traditionally considered any activity that took them away from the study of Torah to be a waste of time. They taught that modesty was an important value—you don't expose the body, you keep it covered up in a respectful way. (Apparently they didn't foresee the evolution of today's bat mitzvah party.) And circumcision is the most vital ritual linking every Jewish male throughout history back to Abraham.

When the Hellenists took over Jerusalem, they wanted to make it clear who was in charge. Leaving no doubt, they proceeded right to the Holy Temple, the center of Jewish worship, and trashed the place. They destroyed or ruined everything they found there, spread pig's blood around (fully realizing the special insult that represented), and erected a statue of Zeus. This was now a holy *Greek* temple.

How do you think the Jews of ancient Israel reacted? Not too strongly, as it turned out. Most went along with the new laws. They embraced Greek culture and stopped practicing Judaism. Some males who wanted to compete in athletic events without the stigma of an altered body even underwent operations to reverse their circumcisions. Now *that's* commitment.

Not everyone went quietly into that Greek night, however. There were Jews who refused to obey the new laws. They risked their lives by observing Jewish rituals and continuing to circumcise their sons. Soon an organized rebellion started to take shape. Mattathius, a high priest formerly of the Temple, and his five sons led a revolt against Antiochus and his policies. Mattathius died soon after, and his son Judah took over as the leader. He quickly became known as *Yehudah HaMacabee*, Judah the Hammer, because he was a mighty force in battle.

Judah and his ragtag band of freedom fighters were horribly outnumbered by the fearsome power of the Greek army. There was no way they should have stood a chance. Yet they were ultimately successful in warding off the might of the opposing army, and they took control of the Temple site. They had won and it was now possible to practice Judaism openly again!

But what did they find when they entered the Temple? A huge mess. This was not something that could be cleaned up in an afternoon. It likely took months of repair and rebuilding. The Greek statues had to be removed, the blood cleaned up, the original Temple apparatus restored, and the whole Temple reconsecrated for religious use.

Finally, the job was completed. Today, if a building were destroyed by fire, let's say, and then rebuilt, the owners might stage a ribbon-cutting ceremony to celebrate their success. The same thing took place two thousand years ago. The high priests rededicated the Temple and declared an eight-day festival to commemorate this wonderful event. In fact, this was such a source of pride and triumph that every year following, the Jews recalled their victory by observing the same eight-day festival of dedication.

Um . . . Did You Forget Something?

Wait, that's it? Is this some kind of discount book—it only includes half the information? How could I leave out the *most important part?*!

That's right. In my story there was not one mention of oil or the miracle of it lasting for eight days.

Let's make a distinction right now between two really important but completely different things: history and religion. To put it as simply as possible, history is a record of events that took place. The Civil War. The fact that Jesus lived and preached. The Maccabees' revolt against Hellenization. The powder-blue tux I wore to my prom. These things happened. They are objective facts, without the effect of religious influence.

Of course, there are many people who don't see it that way. Religious fundamentalists, by definition, consider the Bible to be a literal record of history. This is played out in classrooms and other settings all the time when we're talking about the story of creation as written in Genesis versus scientific knowledge of the Big Bang and evolution. I believe that it's possible to make a distinction between actual historical events and the religious interpretation of those events, and Chanukah is a perfect example of how these two things can differ.

There are certain ancient books that make up what's called the Apocrypha. These are writings that are either historically or religiously important but for a variety of reasons were never included within the canon of the Bible. One such example is the book of Maccabees, which is a historical record of our very own Chanukah story. You might imagine that this would be the authoritative source on what happened and how Jewish history looks upon the events. So it's curious that there's no mention of any miracle concerning the retaking of the Temple. Instead, it chronicles in great detail the rise of the Maccabees and their eventual military victory. It wasn't until hundreds of years later that we read or learn anything having to do with oil or a miracle. Chanukah, meaning "dedication," was simply an eight-day festival celebrated each year after the initial victory to remember and celebrate the Maccabees and the right of the Jews to practice their religion. Not only is there no mention of a super-powered miraculous jar of oil, but no reason is given for the eight-day duration of the festival. We can infer that the length of time was a remembrance of King Solomon and the completion of the First Temple. Since Solomon declared an eight-day feast to celebrate that event, so, too, did the Maccabees when their restoration project was done.

The Miracle, at Last

We need to fast-forward centuries later to the time of the Talmud to find any reference to a miracle. The Talmud is the written record of conversations that the rabbis had while discussing the Mishnah, a body of Jewish law. So they might quote one sentence of the Mishnah, perhaps one law on when to recite a certain prayer, and then talk, argue, and tell stories for page after page. Someone must have taken very good shorthand, because we have the whole discussion and each rabbi's contribution. It's really an incredible glimpse into the lives of people who lived a very long time ago.

Eventually, the rabbis got to the subject of Chanukah. In true rabbinic fashion they led the discussion with the rhetorical question of "What is Chanukah?" and then proceeded to answer it. According to these rabbis, the Jews were able to reclaim the Holy Temple through the miraculous intervention of God. When it was time to rededicate the Temple for ritual use, they went to light the menorah, an item that was always present in the Temple and should be constantly lit. Unfortunately, they were only able to locate one sealed jar of oil, and it would take about eight days for them to prepare and press the olives that would provide them with a new supply. Hoping for the best anyway, they went ahead and lit that oil, which lasted not for one day but for the full eight days they needed before they could replace it. Today, we remember and celebrate that miracle by lighting our own menorahs for the eight-day festival of Chanukah.

Huh? Is it possible that the rabbis had gotten into the Manishewitz that day? How can two versions of the same event be so different? And what was wrong with the original story, anyway? I think it was pretty inspiring that a small but determined force of freedom fighters was able to defeat such a powerful adversary and maintain the practice of Judaism. We know that the Maccabees declared an eight-day festival to remember this event. Why add a story about magic oil?

In order to answer these questions, you have to better understand what the rabbis were thinking about, what was important to them, and the world in which they lived. They weren't dumb. They were well aware of historical events and fashioned this new interpretation for very good reasons.

Reason One: You Can't Have Religion Without God

The original recounting of the military victory, while certainly powerful and engaging, was bereft of any mention of God. This was unacceptable to the rabbis, who sought to reframe the entire back story so that it was God-centered. In their version, it was not the surprising success of the Maccabees that won the day. Instead, it was the intervention and will of God, who led them to victory over the pagan Greeks.

Furthermore, it wasn't just an arbitrary declaration of an eight-day festival, but rather a miracle (by definition, something produced by God) that formed the basis of the holiday. This is one way in which historic events (military victory) can be expressed through the perspective of religion (miracle). Both are equally vital within the Jewish tradition.

Reason Two: It's All About the Ratings

Pretend you're a screenwriter and you have to pitch a blockbuster script. Something that will be enjoyed for generations to come. You've come up with two drafts. The first tells a fairly good war story. Small, underdog group of fighters. Victorious against all odds. Some exciting action sequences and a fair amount of violence. Not bad. That might sell pretty well. I bet viewers would pay money to watch that movie.

The second version includes the victory but also incorporates special effects. First we witness the might of God, guiding the soldiers. Then, after God ensures the Jews' victory over the powerful enemy, He miraculously transforms one small, lonely jar of oil into an eight-day-long beacon of divine intervention as His people rededicate the Holy Temple. The worshippers behold God's holy might in awe. Wow!

Which screenplay is likely to sell? Which one do the producers think has much greater potential to pack viewers in their seats and become a classic for years after?

The rabbis figured all this out a long time ago. The historic facts of Chanukah made for interesting but not amazing reading. If the holiday had only been about a military victory, it would likely have been commemorated each year and eventually forgotten, probably after a modest number of generations. There just wasn't enough *oomph* there. But when coupled with an incredible narrative of God and a miracle, well, now you've got yourself a story that will be passed down through the years. This version also appeals to the kids, and all good producers know that when the kids are hooked, you've also got the parents. In addition to their very real concern about including God in the tale, the rabbis were cognizant of the fact that they needed to infuse this holiday with some more staying power. They accomplished this by incorporating the now familiar legend of the miracle.

Reason Three: Don't Make a Fuss

There's a poignant Jewish joke that tells about two Jews facing execution for practicing Judaism despite their government's persecution. As they're both lined up before the firing squad, the soldier tells them that they may each say some last words.

The first Jew declares, "I fight to my last breath this corrupt and godless government, and I assert my eternal commitment to being Jewish!"

The second Jew leans over and whispers, "Morty, shhh. Don't make a fuss."

Throughout history, Jews have lived with the very real and terrifying threat of persecution. If they were lucky, the government of their host country tolerated them. They were allowed to be Jewish, have their distinct practices, and go about their business without anyone really bothering them too much. But at other times, Jews were punished and tortured for practicing their religion. This idea of blending into the background, not causing a fuss, and hoping to just be left alone was a genuine and justifiable reality.

Now here comes Chanukah with its loud and bombastic message of Jews rising up in revolt and overthrowing a powerful government! The Talmudic rabbis living in Roman times certainly did not want to emphasize this theme of the events. Doing so could have been dangerous, making the government nervous and possibly leading to more persecution of Jews. Instead, the rabbis composed a version of the Chanukah story that preserved the most important elements of the events but highlighted an innocuous divine miracle.

Reason Four: The Benefit of Hindsight

Because the rabbis lived hundreds of years after the events of Chanukah took place, they had a different perspective. Sure, we know all about the Maccabees' incredible victory and the Jewish retaking of the Temple. But what happened after that?

The family of Judah the Maccabee established themselves as the leaders of this new Jewish government. They were known as the Hasmonean (or, in Hebrew, *Chashmona'im*) dynasty. Judah's descendants were the new leaders. In an ironic twist, the Hasmonean dynasty ended up succumbing to the very enemy they had been fighting against—Hellenization. The Hasmoneans included many men with Greek names, and the dynasty itself soon became completely Hellenized. The Hasmoneans only ruled for a hundred or so years. To the rabbis who knew the outcome of the Maccabee victory, the Hasmoneans were not the greatest role models. As a result, they sought to take a lot of the story's focus off these flawed warriors.

The Christmas Connection

I imagine that countless Hebrew school kids and parents have been reminded each year not to turn Chanukah into the Jewish Christmas. We're told that it's only because the two holidays are so close to each other on the calendar that we even need to have this conversation. We are also taught that some of the customs of Christmas, such as giving gifts, have migrated to Chanukah but that the two holidays have no real connection.

Well, yes and no. These two disparate holidays, as far apart in their sacred meaning as could be, actually do share a connection with each other. To find out more, we need to go way back in time.

Imagine a person living in ancient times, before technology or industry. There's no common understanding of how the world works or the passage of time. He lives. He farms. He eats. He fights for survival. Eventually he dies. Over the course of time, while he's farming and eating the food that he grows, he starts to notice that it's getting colder. He also observes that it seems to be getting darker too. Each day that passes feels colder and darker.

We know what's happening, of course. Winter's coming. The days are getting shorter. A lot of people dread winter or suffer from seasonal affective disorder. But we also realize that if we just wait it out, it'll start to warm up again pretty soon and the days will begin to get longer. In fact, right around the first day of winter, also known as the winter solstice, the day is at its shortest. All days after that, even in the dead of winter, are actually getting a bit longer. Soon it will be spring and we can walk around outside in comfort again.

That's how modern people think because we understand how the calendar works, and we know that the earth tilts on its axis and revolves around the sun, giving us two opposite solstices and explaining why countless Jews migrate to Florida each winter. But in ancient times, however, our imaginary person has no idea about any of that. All he knows is that sun seems to be going away and that his life may be imminent danger. Perhaps the sun is angry at him! He will pray to the god of the sun so that the heat and light return. Ancient pagans would engage in something called "sympathetic magic." It was the way that a person would demonstrate to a god what they were praying for. For instance, if someone was praying for rain, he might take a barrel full of water, throw it up in the air, and watch it all rain down on the earth as if to say, "Here! This is what we need. Please give us *this*!"

And so it was with praying for warmth and light. Ancient worshippers would light fires to show their gods what they needed. They probably lit lots of things on fire and created quite a display. Pagans were also known to engage in human sacrifice to assuage their gods.

C HRISTMAS HAS a similar historical background to Chanukah. Early Christian leaders were also unhappy with pagan solstice festivals. They, too, connected an important religious event in
their own calendar to that time of year—namely, the sacred birth
of Jesus. It's no accident that both Christmas and Chanukah, one
sacred and the other relatively minor, both include symbols of light
in their celebration.

After all the praying and sacrifice and fires, the people might then
declare a festival, which was probably worse than any college frat party
you could imagine. And all of this took place right around the winter
solstice every year.

Enter the Israelites and Judaism, as they took their place alongside
the indigenous pagans. It soon became common for them to celebrate
a winter festival with their neighbors. As Judaism was being formed
and its rituals solidified, this behavior was viewed as unacceptable.
One of the defining tenets of being Jewish was specifically *not* to
engage in the pagan customs, sacrifice, or cult worship. And yet it was
hard to get them to stop.

So instead, in a brilliant feat of "if you can't beat 'em, join 'em,"
the rabbis *connected* this stubborn winter festival with an existing
eight-day holiday whose years were probably numbered anyway. They
turned a slightly ho-hum festival of dedication into a much more
exciting Festival of Lights. In the process, they very cleverly transformed the pagan practice of lighting fires into an integral part of
Chanukah's identity.

The Menorah

The menorah, strictly speaking, has nothing to do with Chanukah.
There were several distinct articles found in the Holy Temple that

were used on a regular basis. There was the altar, where animals were sacrificed. There was the special holy section set off by a curtain that was known as the Holy of Holies, which was entered only by the high priest on Yom Kippur. And then there was the menorah. It didn't look exactly the way you're probably picturing it. It was a seven-branched candelabrum, and it was kept lit throughout the week.

The rabbis seized on this one ritual item and described the high priests as having only a small amount of oil on hand with which to keep it lit. In this way, the menorah became associated with Chanukah. Because the traditional Temple menorah only had seven branches, a new, improved Chanukah menorah came into existence, called a *chanukiyah*. If you look closely, you'll notice that every modern-day *chanukiyah* (or we can just go back to calling them menorahs like everyone else does) holds nine candles. Why? Doesn't Chanukah have *eight* days? Can't *something* be simple for a change?

Chanukah candles are considered holy, in that their only purpose is to commemorate the holiday and the miracle. Go back not too long ago before electricity was common, and you can imagine that a lit menorah would also make a handy source of light for the room, even though you're not supposed to use it for that purpose. But how can you look at candles burning brightly in a dark room and *not* use the light?

That's why we have the extra candle. Each evening, we light not only the specific number of candles that are required but also another candle, called the *shammash*, so that we can tell ourselves that any benefit that we're getting from the light is coming from *that* candle, not the actual Chanukah candles. Pretty clever.

Come On Baby, Light My Fire

In Talmudic times, the rabbis couldn't even agree on how to light the menorah. Remember that until they declared that the dedication festival known as Chanukah was now to be connected to a miracle of oil and be known as the Festival of Lights, no one was lighting any *chanukiyah* or menorah. So not only did they have to initiate the requirement to light, they also needed to prescribe the proper way to do so.

Eight nights. Should we light the menorah completely each evening? Should we light a different number of candles each night? Does it matter in which direction we place the candles? Should any particular candle be lit first? For that matter, do all menorahs have to look the same? Do we put the menorah in a special place, or can it go anywhere? The rabbis had to come up with answers to all these questions.

In the Talmud, we often read about two distinct groups of rabbis—those who belonged to the school of Hillel, and others from the school of Shammai. Which one do you think prevailed most of the time? Have you ever heard of Shammai? I didn't think so. Shammai and his followers declared that one should light the entire menorah on the first night of Chanukah, and each subsequent evening take one candle away, so that on the last night, just one candle is burning. Conversely, the school of Hillel directed us to start with one candle and add another one each night, finishing the eighth day of Chanukah with a full menorah.

I suppose that the Hillel-ites and Shammai-ites squared off in the parking lot of the Talmudic headquarters in some ancient version of *West Side Story*. But we all know how that ended up. All the other rabbis of the Talmud ruled in favor of the school of Hillel, explaining very sensibly that if the Chanukah candles are holy, then we should be adding holiness each night of the holiday, not taking it away.

Furthermore, they continued to lay out all the specific details that later generations would need. Candles are placed from right to left, but when you light the candles you go from left to right so that the newest candle is lit first. A menorah may be made out of any material, but each one of the eight candles should be the same height, so that one night is not given more importance than the others. While it doesn't necessarily have to be straight, a menorah shouldn't be circular, because then it would be hard to tell which candle corresponds to which night of Chanukah.

Finally, it's traditional to place the menorah near a window so that it's visible from the outside. This fulfills another important commandment, known as *pirsumei nisah*, or "publicizing the miracle." The rabbis of the Talmud wanted to emphasize the power of God and the miracle of the oil by making it visible to as many passersby as possible.

Keep the menorah away from any curtains, though, or you'll get a lot more publicity than you need.

You Will Be Assimilated

One of the most central and significant themes of Chanukah is the fight against assimilation. The Maccabees fought against the Greek army and their laws of Hellenization. They went to battle and were eventually victorious in maintaining the Jewish people's right to worship and to preserve their religion and distinct identity and culture. It's pretty ironic, then, that throughout the years Chanukah has borrowed a large number of customs from other cultures and religions. On the very holiday that we celebrate our people's resistance to blending in with those around them, a lot of the familiar rituals actually come from other countries throughout different time periods.

Let's Take a Spin

Is there any more familiar and beloved symbol of Chanukah than the simple dreidl? If not for this one piece of Chanukana, music teachers in every public school in America would have no idea how to include any Chanukah music in their winter concerts and make the parents of their Jewish students happy.

The dreidl is a four-sided top, with a Hebrew letter on each side. The four Hebrew letters are *Nun, Gimmel, Hei,* and *Shin.* Those letters stand for the Hebrew words *Nes Gadol Hayah Sham,* meaning "A great miracle happened there." (Dreidls manufactured in Israel have a different last letter, the letter *Pay,* standing for the Hebrew word *Po,* so that its message reads, "A great miracle happened *here.*")

Playing dreidl is a form of gambling in which each letter represents a particular action.

Nun, indicating *Nisht* (nothing): The next person spins.
Gimmel, indicating *Gantze* (all): You take everything in the pot.
Hei, indicating *Halb* (half): You get half the pot.
Shin, indicating *Shtel* (put): Put one coin (or whatever you're playing for) in the pot.

Notice that the results the Hebrew letters indicate are Yiddish words, which gives us a clue as to the origin of this game.

According to Chanukah lore, after the Greeks had outlawed the practice of Judaism, some Jews would secretly study Torah, often hiding out in remote locations to do so. When they heard the approach of government troops, they would quickly hide their texts and whip out their dreidls. Apparently, the mighty Greek army was easily fooled into thinking that large numbers of their citizens were sitting in distant fields so that they could spin tops together. "OK, folks, you carry on with that fun game. Let us know if you see any *Jews* out here."

In fact, the dreidl was a common toy found in many European countries since the 1500s. Our familiar game of dreidl most closely resembles a German version in which a four-sided top called a *trundl* was spun. It, too, had the same four actions—the German words for each letter on the *trundl* were pretty much the same as the Yiddish words.

Grace Me with Your Presents

So what do you think? Is the modern-day custom of exchanging Chanukah presents something new? Or has it always been done? Is it just something that American Jews picked up from their non-Jewish neighbors because of Christmas?

Yes. No. All of the above.

There is no doubt that the way we shop for and give Chanukah presents to each other, and especially to our kids, is borrowed from what is going on around us during this time of year. Retailers are more than happy to increase their consumer base to include not only those celebrating Christmas but also Jewish customers who want to do what all of their neighbors are doing. It turns out, however, that giving gifts on Chanukah really does have a rich history of its own.

Jews would often give gifts of coins, better known as *Chanukah gelt*. Chanukah, above all else, is a holiday that commemorated the Maccabees' taking control of Jerusalem. Before the modern state of Israel came into being in 1948, the time of the Maccabees was the last time the Jews controlled their own government. And what represents nationalism more than currency and coins? By giving and exchanging coins, Jews were marking the triumph of the Maccabees and celebrating Jewish control of the Land of Israel. Even today, we still practice this custom with those ubiquitous chocolate coins, always wrapped in gold foil and mysteriously housed in yellow netting.

In this country, *Chanukah gelt* eventually got replaced by non-monetary presents, since the vast majority of people were buying and giving them already. There are still a lot of Jews who like to give *Chanukah gelt*, and lots of kids who are more than happy to receive money rather than a sweater that they'll never wear.

Play the Funky Music

Nothing warms this cantor's heart more than the beautiful music of Chanukah, telling of the warmth and love of this holiday and how our families cherish this sacred holiday by gathering at home, basking in our devotion to each other.

OK, this might be overdoing it a bit.

In fact, there would be little Chanukah music at all if the holiday didn't have to compete with Christmas, which has an immense collection of traditional and classic music. We have "Rock of Ages" and "The Dreidl Song," while the list of traditional Christmas carols seems endless.

There has been a lot of what I call faux-Chanukah music written in recent years. These songs describe Chanukah as a Christmas-like holiday celebrated by Jews. Just as on Christmas, families supposedly gather at home (and you can just picture the logs in the fireplace burning), and there are the ubiquitous themes of peace, light, and love. The only places these songs are actually sung are in public school winter concerts. These songs, while well-meaning, completely miss the point of Chanukah. Rather than celebrating peace and love, Chanukah remembers a bloody and violent military overthrow of a powerful government. Traditional Chanukah songs deal with Judah the mighty warrior or the powerful hand of God. They might also discuss the miracle of the oil and the light that lasted eight days.

Sometimes a song proves to be so popular that it exists simultaneously in various languages. "Chanukah O Chanukah" is an example of a well-known song that is sung in Yiddish, Hebrew, and English. While each version is pretty close to the others, they are not direct translations.

Here is the Yiddish version:

Chanukah oy Chanukah, a yontif a sheyner,
A lustiker a freylekher nisht do nokh azoyner
Ale nakht mit dreydlech shpiln mir,
Frishe heyse latkes, esn on a shir.

Here is the English translation of the Yiddish version:

Chanukah oh Chanukah, a beautiful holiday.
A cheerful and joyous one, there is none like it.
Every night we will play with the dreidls,
Fresh, hot latkes we will eat endlessly.

Maybe it's just me, but I think everything sounds better in Yiddish. I picture this version of the song like a movie in black and white, dripping with *schmaltz* (literally, "chicken fat," but also meaning "over-the-top sappiness") and nostalgia. This is the sort of song sung by a *bubbe* (a Jewish grandmother) wearing an apron while she prepares enough potato latkes to feed the entire *shtetl*.

Compare this with the Hebrew version of this song:

Yemei hachanuka chanukat mikdasheinu
Begil uvesimcha memalim et libeinu
Laila vayom svivoneinu yisov
Suvganiot nochal gam larov

In English, the Hebrew version would read,

The days of Chanukah, the dedication of our Holy Temple,
With joy and happiness we will fill our hearts.
Day and night we'll spin our dreidls
And we'll also eat many doughnuts.

No, that wasn't a typo. The song says doughnuts. As I'll point out a little later on, in Israel doughnuts are more traditional for Chanukah than latkes. It's also noteworthy that this text mentions the dedication of the Holy Temple, which is the historical reason for Chanukah.

Finally, we have the English version of the song:

Hanukah, Oh Hanukah come light the menorah
Let's have a party we'll all dance the horah
Gather 'round the table, we'll give you a treat
Dreidls to play with, and latkes to eat.

I can tell you that I've never heard of even one family that spontaneously broke into a *horah* (a type of ring dance) after lighting the Chanukah candles. You can see that while there are definitely similarities among all three versions, each one is still distinct in its own right, and each highlights a different aspect of the festival.

No section on Chanukah music would be complete without a mention of what's become the traditional anthem of the holiday, "Maoz Tzur," also known in English by the more famous title "Rock of Ages." This, too, has both a Hebrew and an English version. Above all others, this song is associated most directly with Chanukah. Its most traditional tune is an old German folk melody. The complete text of Maoz Tzur is a six-stanza-long epic poem detailing God's salvation of the Jewish people throughout history. Only the first stanza is commonly sung. Compare the following words with modern Chanukah songs about love and family:

Ma'oz tzur yeshu'ati, lekha na'eh leshabe'ah.
Tikon beit tefilati, vesham toda nezabe'ah.
Le'et takhin matbe'ah mitzor hamnabe'ah.
Az egmor beshir mizmor hanukat hamizbe'ah.

[My refuge and my rock of salvation, it is pleasant to sing Your praises.
Let our house of prayer be restored. And there we will offer You our thanks.
When You will have slaughtered the blaspheming enemy,
Then we will celebrate with song and psalms the dedication of the altar.]

I dare you to find *that* on a Hallmark card. Maoz Tzur, with its military imagery and mention of the Temple's altar, is a much more appropriate song for Chanukah, and it's a lot more consistent with the holiday's background.

Let's Eat

The potato pancake, or latke, is one of the most identifiably Jewish foods. It takes its place right next to gefilte fish as the classic Jewish fare. In fact, non-Jewish people think that these foods are the only things we ever eat. If you go into a supermarket on *any* Jewish holiday, you will find three things on sale every time: gefilte fish, potato latkes, and grape juice. Now *there's* an interesting meal.

On Chanukah, it's traditional to eat foods prepared in oil in order to further celebrate the miracle and to help your cardiologist make another payment on his condo in Scottsdale. It's too bad that the Chanukah story is popularized most often with fried potato pancakes and not some healthy vegetables sautéed lightly in olive oil.

Like so many of the other customs associated with Chanukah, potato latkes are a product of a later time. Potatoes were not commonly found in ancient times, but they became a staple of Jewish cooking in later years when the Jews lived throughout Europe. Potatoes were cheap and plentiful. It's also likely that latkes (a Yiddish word) were something that were prepared and enjoyed throughout the year. Generations of Jewish mothers and grandmothers scraped their knuckles grating pounds of potatoes by hand and splattered burning oil all over themselves and every inch of their kitchens. Now at least we have food processors.

In Israel it's not latkes, but rather *sufganiyot*, doughnuts, most often filled with jelly, that are the most popular holiday food. Rather than the usual round doughnut that we're used to eating with our coffee, these are usually small, deep-fried balls of dough, most often infused with jelly filling, based on a common food from North Africa. Again, this is an example of a traditional holiday food coming from the host cultures of where Jews used to live.

Certainly our ancestors never heard of another popular term associated with Chanukah: cholesterol.

The Bottom Line

Chanukah comprises a number of contradictions. It is a minor festival that has risen to great prominence in the Jewish calendar and in Jewish homes. It is a holiday that celebrates the Jewish people's resistance to assimilation. At the same time, most of its customs and traditions are borrowed from the various cultures in which the Jews have lived. The holiday that teaches us to resist assimilation is largely a product of it.

You might notice that in this chapter, I did not include any section labeled "Perfect for Families." In fact, Chanukah is centered entirely around the home. Its rituals and traditions are observed by families at home. There are a couple of things that are done in temple, mainly adding a couple of prayers to the regular service. But lighting the menorah, cooking special foods, playing dreidl, and giving gifts (monetary or otherwise) are all things that families do together at home.

What's old is new. The Greeks told the Jews not to practice their religion and to participate in athletic competitions instead. In countless synagogues, the exact same struggle continues, as families and kids have scheduled sports events when services are taking place. Chanukah's two-thousand-year-old message still resonates today.

CHAPTER 6

PURIM

THE ULTIMATE JEWISH
REVENGE FANTASY

NOTHING SAYS fun for the kids like attempted genocide.
While you may have a passing familiarity with our old
stand-by characters Queen Esther, Mordechai, and Haman,
as well as the custom of kids dressing up, there's a lot more going on
here. As with all the other holidays, let's take a peek behind the curtain
and find out what Purim is really about. I bet you'll be surprised by
what you discover.

The Back Story

The entire story of Purim is based on the book (sometimes called the
scroll) of Esther, found in the *Ketuvim*, or Writings section of the

Bible. It chronicles a time when the Jews lived in Persia under the reign of King Achashverosh. Whether this was an actual king, based on an actual king, or a historical event at all is really beside the point. What's most important is the action that takes place in this story.

First, you should know that the book of Esther is one of the finest short stories that you'll ever read. It has everything. Action. Intrigue. Sex. Violence. Conflict. Character development. A turning point. Foreshadowing. Suspense. Irony. Climax. Resolution. They should assign this to be read in schools so that the teacher can point out the beauty of each literary technique.

Because this story has a sense of humor and doesn't take itself quite so seriously, I imagine the ancient rabbis had themselves a merry old time when they got their hands on this scroll and decided to include it in the canon of the Hebrew Bible. I can picture them sitting around a big table, on their third or fourth schnapps of the afternoon. One of them asks, "So what do you think, guys, should Esther make it in?" And all the other rabbis raise their cups and respond, "Yeah!" (Then they wake up the next morning, look at each other, and say, "We did *what*?")

Let's take a nice close look at the story, and try to get beyond what you learned in first grade: Haman—bad. Mordechai—good. Esther—pretty. There's way more going on.

We are introduced to King Achashverosh and told that he rules a huge area, with the city of Shushan as the capital. The scene opens on the king holding a party. This is not an intimate dinner party for a few close friends. Rather, this shindig lasts seven days and includes many people who live in and around the palace. The king's wife, Vashti, is having a soiree of her own for all of her lady friends, and that, too, is going on for seven days.

On the seventh day the king and all of his guests are pretty sloshed, and, as guys have been known to do from time to time, they start comparing wives. The king declares that his wife is the best-looking (and really, who's going to argue with the king?) and summons Vashti to come out and strut her stuff in front of the other men. We now meet Judaism's very first feminist. Vashti refuses! She finds the whole idea to be demeaning. I'm not sure that anyone had ever said no to

Achashverosh before. He is livid and probably somewhat embarrassed in front of his underlings, but he remains quiet.

The other men, though, see the writing on the wall (to completely mix biblical metaphors) and push the matter with the king. How will it look, they ask, if word gets around that the king's own wife refused his command and nothing happened to her? You'll have women saying "No" to their husbands throughout the entire kingdom! The horror!

King Achashverosh agrees with this reasoning. So he declares that as a result of her blatant disobedience, Vashti will be . . .

What? What happens? If you think you know this story, can you tell me what becomes of Vashti? Nine out of ten Jews will respond that Vashti is executed, probably by beheading. (The tenth Jew has snuck out of the sanctuary and gotten a head start on the bagels.)

But according to the text, that's not actually what happens. Instead, Vashti is simply banished from the kingdom. We don't know her fate, other than that she is forbidden from ever appearing in front of Achashverosh again. Perhaps she moved to Vermont with a friend to open up an art gallery. Just in case all the women in the kingdom didn't get the hint, the king further decrees that all men will be the ultimate authority in their households. So there.

The king now needs a new wife.

This is a perfect time for the text to introduce us to our next major character—a Jew named Mordechai who is descended from the tribe of Benjamin.

Mordechai has a cousin named Hadassah, who also goes by the name Esther, something much less Jewish-sounding in those days. In many translations and versions of this story, we are told that Mordechai is Esther's uncle. Given the way the action will unfold, that would be a little creepy. I've always felt that Mordechai was just a little bit off—maybe there was a second scroll about him that was never made public.

Now, if you need to meet a potential spouse, there are different ways to go about accomplishing that. You might try the bar scene, take out a personal ad, or even go on JDate. But if you're the king of the entire land, those methods are a little too mundane. Instead, you hold an immense beauty contest and have all the eligible females parade in front of you for your approval.

Mordechai enters his cousin (or his niece? . . . see, I told you: creepy) in this beauty pageant and tells her not to let anyone know she's Jewish.

I wonder who ends up winning the beauty contest.

Spoiler alert: Esther wins!

She becomes Queen Esther, and Mordechai has successfully married off his teenage cousin or niece to a rich, middle-aged, non-Jewish guy.

Then we read what seems to be a throwaway incident. Mordechai is hanging around the palace when he overhears two palace guards, Bigtan and Teresh, plotting to kill the king. He calls 911 and reports what he found out. The plot is foiled and Mordechai is appropriately given credit in the royal chronicles.

Time for the text to insert the first element of conflict, in the person of a man named Haman. We don't know where he came from before this chapter. We just know that he became the king's favorite guy and that he's descended from the tribe of Agag. The king likes and trusts Haman so much that he removes the signet ring from his own finger and gives it to Haman. In other words, Haman now has complete power of attorney. He can do, decree, or proclaim almost anything he wants in the king's name. The only person more powerful than Haman is Achashverosh himself.

One day, Haman is out and about, enjoying the fear that he engenders in the people who see him. It has become the custom for everyone to lower their faces and bow down as Haman passes by. However, Mordechai refuses to do so. The royal guards try to convince him to just go along and not make a fuss, but Mordechai is adamant about not bowing down to Haman.

Some words of explanation here: Most people consider Mordechai's actions to be brave and valiant. After all, we're taught that Jews only bow down to God. But the way I read the story, that's not really what's going on here. I would imagine the "bowing" looked more like the Japanese custom, which is an act of courtesy and respect, rather than getting down on one's knees and prostrating low on the ground. For some reason Mordechai is the only person who seems to resent Haman's presence and wants to show him disrespect. We certainly find out soon enough that Haman is an archvillain, but until now we've read or learned nothing about him that would indicate any reason why Mordechai shouldn't like him.

I've always wondered what might have happened if Mordechai had simply swallowed his pride and lowered his face in the presence of Haman. Perhaps all the unpleasantness that followed could have been avoided.

Instead, Haman sees that this guy is being outwardly disrespectful to him, and he wants to learn more about him. Who is he? Where is he from?

Haman learns that Mordechai is a Jew and, like a typical anti-Semite, Haman decides that he hates all Jews because they're not like him and their ways and customs are different. He figures that while it would be great to kill Mordechai, it would be even better to simply eliminate his entire race.

Something this big needs royal approval, so Haman appears before the king (with tribute money in hand, just in case) and says offhandedly, "Hey, there are these people in your kingdom whose ways are really strange and objectionable to me. Would you mind if I wiped them all out?"

King Achashverosh, not exactly the picture of hands-on leadership, responds, "Yeah, sure, whatever."

Haman is thrilled, and he and his wife Zeresh draw lots (in Hebrew, *purim*) to decide on the date when Mordechai will be hanged and the Jewish people wiped out.

Word gets back to Mordechai, who one could possibly argue was the cause of all this trouble in the first place. He and Esther share the news among all the Jews, and they declare a three-day fast. Mordechai urges Esther to go before the king and plead the Jewish people's case.

Not so fast.

Even if you're married to the guy, you don't just walk up to a king and start a conversation. There are rules for these things. You have to be summoned. So Esther, literally taking her life in her hands, tentatively approaches Achashverosh and cautiously asks if she may have an audience with him.

Luck is on her side; the king is in a great mood. "What is it, my dear? Anything you want, just name it."

She tells him that she is planning a party and asks would he please honor everyone with his presence. The king responds, "Of course, and be sure to tell Haman and Zeresh too, so they can be there."

During this party, Esther announces that she's having such a great time, she'd like to have *another* party later in the week, and would everyone please come to that one too.

I'd love to live in Shushan. All they do is have wild parties and beauty contests.

Now comes the turning point of the whole story.

The king is lying in bed late one night, suffering from a royal case of insomnia. Whereas you or I might pick up a book and try reading, the king has people for that. So he summons his servants and has them read to him from the royal chronicles. Right there in the police log is the story of how Mordechai turned in a couple of would-be assassins and saved the king's life.

The king interrupts the reading. He asks, "What did we ever do to reward Mordechai for his actions?" He finds out that nothing was ever done. "Well, this won't do. We need to recognize his loyalty. I wonder what we should do."

At that very moment, Haman happens to walk by the royal chamber. Achashverosh stops him and asks, "Haman, if there was someone that I wanted to reward greatly for his wonderful service to me, what do you think I should do?"

This next part would make any sitcom writer proud. In a fit of wacky misunderstanding, Haman thinks to himself, "Why, the king must be talking about *me*! I'd better play this cool."

Haman chortles to himself and responds that the king should dress this person in royal purple robes, put him on the best white horse, and parade him through town, announcing to all, "This is the man the king wishes to reward."

The king thinks that this all sounds just dandy, and says, "Make it so. This is what we're going to do for Mordechai!"

Haman is devastated, angry, and starting to get nervous, but he knows that he has the king's decree to eliminate the Jews in his back pocket.

Later that week, everyone assembles again at Esther's second party. As before, Esther takes a chance and asks to speak to the king. And once again, he is gracious and receptive to anything she'd like. Now she drops the bombshell. "My king, I am Jewish. There is a bad man who wishes to kill me, Mordechai, and our entire people."

Achashverosh is incensed! "Who would plan such an insidious plot?"

Esther points dramatically right at Haman. "*That man!*"

The king is filled with rage at Haman and leaves momentarily. Haman, overcome with desperation, pleads with Esther for his life and even begins to faint, pretty much landing prone on top of her. This is when the king returns, looks upon this scene, and drily delivers one of the best one-liners in biblical history: "Oh, so you thought you'd also have your way with my wife."

Haman's plot is officially foiled. But we don't get the happy ending yet. Remember that Haman distributed the king's original decree allowing all the people in the kingdom to eliminate the Jews among them. Even if the king later changes his mind, his decree still carries the weight of the law. King Achashverosh comes up with a workaround. He issues another decree—this one giving the Jews permission to defend themselves and fight against their attackers. So the Jews hang Haman on the very gallows that he had built for Mordechai. And for good measure, they kill Haman's ten sons (who were also a bunch of no-goodniks).

Not enough revenge for you? In a passage worthy of a Quentin Tarantino film, the Jews continue to defend themselves against their enemies, wiping out seventy-five thousand people who were bent on their destruction. But they do not take any spoils or plunder. So that's not so bad.

That'll teach you to mess with the Jews.

The epilogue of the story tells us that from that day forward, this whole affair will be commemorated every year with the holiday of Purim. It is to be a time of celebration and merry-making. Jews should also give to the poor and exchange gifts of food with one another.

The Back Back Story

Remember that the text went out of its way early on to tell us from which tribes both Mordechai and Haman were descended. That was no accident.

Back in the book of Samuel, we read about King Saul, a rather sad, pathetic, and probably manic-depressive king of Israel. King Saul is commanded by God to completely and utterly wipe out the entire tribe of Amalek, always represented in the Bible as the archenemy of the Israelite people. King Saul is to order his soldiers to kill every man, woman, child, and even animal of this tribe. Don't take spoils. Spare no one. Combatant, noncombatant—it doesn't matter. Everyone and everything is to be destroyed. To be sure, this is a problematic passage of the Bible and very difficult for modern readers to understand.

King Saul obviously has similar misgivings. He *almost* carries out God's command, but he has his soldiers spare the life of Agag, the Amalekite king. This is not so far-fetched. In ancient times, it was common for a conquering king to spare the life of the defeated king. Call it professional courtesy.

God is enraged that King Saul did not obey His direct order and ends up removing Saul and his family from the Israelite royal dynasty. Saul lives out the rest of his life as a failed leader. King Agag is eventually put to death, but we assume that in the time between his capture and his execution, he had time for a conjugal visit and was able to sire a child and begin a line of descendants.

Interesting story, but what does this have to do with Purim?

King Saul was from the tribe of Benjamin. Mordechai was also from the tribe of Benjamin. The Amalekite king was named Agag. Haman was descended from the tribe of Agag. That's right—the entire story of Purim is an *epic rematch*. It's a brilliantly written sequel to an important episode that took place years before. It also informs us that, but for King Saul's disobedience to God's command, there never would have been a Haman.

When knowledgeable and learned scholars of the Bible started reading the book of Esther and they came across these seemingly random details about Mordechai's and Haman's lineage, they immediately understood the significance and realized that this was the Israelites versus their nemeses, the Amalekites, all over again. This back story accomplishes two important things: first, it adds immensely to the reader's enjoyment of the Esther story and, second, it puts the story into a larger context. Instead of being a superb but stand-alone narrative, it also functions as a bridge between two different biblical time periods.

Traditions for the Family

If you attend synagogue for a Purim service, be prepared: it will look like you wandered into a Halloween party. In fact, Purim is sometimes (erroneously) referred to as the "Jewish Halloween."

Because Purim is likely to fall during the week (and it never takes place on Shabbat), the evening service has become a popular time for families to attend because by that time all family members are likely to be home from work and school. Depending on your temple, there may be a morning service as well, especially if Purim falls on a Sunday.

Purim has developed into a child-centered holiday—we encourage kids to dress in costumes. While you'll always see little girls dressed as Queen Esther and boys in Haman or Mordechai costumes, really anything goes. Adults who enjoy getting dressed up can also take the opportunity to be creative.

During the Purim service the scroll (in Hebrew, *megillah*) of Esther is chanted out loud using a special tune that's used only for this purpose. One of the obligations on Purim is for all those in attendance to hear every word of the *megillah* reading.

This presents a problem for a couple of reasons. First, while the entire *megillah* is not particularly long, you have a temple filled with screaming kids in costumes who are able to sense the platters of sweets and other assorted goodies that are already waiting for them in the social hall. The last thing they are likely to do is to sit quietly and listen to the Hebrew chanting.

Second, one of the most famous traditions of Purim is for everyone to make noise each time the name *Haman* is read. We are told to blot out the name of Ham . . . uh, I mean *that guy* forever. So as if hyped-up, costumed, and hungry little kids weren't bad enough, we actually give them noise makers (often referred to by the Yiddish term *groggers*) that they're supposed to use every time they hear a certain name. If you're a migraine sufferer, you might consider an alternate activity this evening.

E VEN WITH all the noise and antsy, sugared-up children, don't hesitate for a moment to bring all family members to a Purim service. Many synagogues will conduct an abbreviated *megillah* reading for young children and their families, incorporating all the fun of making noise over Haman's name and dressing up in costumes. The service will be kept short to help accommodate shorter attention spans.

Wait, it gets worse. Haman's name doesn't even come up until the third chapter. So you can imagine how difficult it is for those in attendance to remain quiet enough for the congregation (those that are paying attention) to hear and discern the words of the *megillah*.

Finally, when the third chapter begins, Haman's name is mentioned pretty frequently. He is, after all, a main character. As soon as the *megillah* reader begins to pronounce the name, everyone is supposed to make as much noise as possible, using their *groggers* or anything else they can think of: yelling "boo" loudly, blowing trumpets, even sounding air horns. This is the one time that no one is likely to *shush* you if your cell phone goes off during services.

One interesting custom that's not done much anymore is to write the name "Haman" on the bottom of your shoes and stamp your feet each time you hear it. You might be aware that insults using the feet or shoes are a particularly strong way of demonstrating contempt in certain parts of the world, so that's probably the origin of this custom.

A Tradition Probably Not for the Family

Another custom on Purim is to get so completely drunk that you are unable to tell the difference between the hero Mordechai and the villain Haman. The actual name for this lovely tradition is the Hebrew phrase *ad lo yada*, which means "until you don't know [the

THERE IS one passage in the book of Deuteronomy that serves as the basis for the entire ritual of drowning out Haman's name.

Throughout the Israelites' wandering in the desert, they occasionally came up against the tribe of Amalek. While it wasn't particularly uncommon for them to go to war against other tribes, the tribe of Amalek was always portrayed as a special case. They were the worst of the worst. Instead of fighting in the usual way, head to head, they would sneak around and attack the Israelites from the rear of their formation—typically where the women, children, and weakest members of the tribe would be found.

So while the Israelites were routinely commanded to fight and vanquish other nations, they were told to go even further with the tribe of Amalek. According to Deuteronomy, we are ordered to always remember what Amalek did to us in the desert, and to extinguish this tribe's name from existence.

While the intent of the edict is pretty clear, I think that the author might have benefited from a good editor. In this passage, the first verse says, "Remember what Amalek did to you." Then two verses later it tells us to "blot out the memory of Amalek from under the heavens."

Well, which is it? Remember? Blot out the memory? Should I remember to get rid of the remembrance? If I successfully blot out the memory, how can I remember what Amalek did?

For good measure, the next phrase says, "Do not forget!"

Oh good, that cleared it up.

In any case, we convert this slightly confusing syntax into the custom of making a huge amount of noise every time we hear the name of Haman during the reading of the Purim story.

difference]." In Israel, the holiday of Purim can resemble Mardi Gras. In many cities, there's a parade (appropriately called the *Ad Lo Yada* Parade), complete with music, flamboyant costumes, and lots of public imbibing.

Synagogue services might also include some schnapps or other similar beverage for adult members of the congregation to enjoy. Most people would certainly agree, however, that any drinking that takes place should be done responsibly and sensibly. Modern rabbis have also determined that one need not take *ad lo yada* too literally.

The Play's the Thing

So far we have lots of people in costumes, a ton of noise, and a fair amount of drinking going on. What could make this even better? I know, let's get on stage and perform.

One of the more entertaining customs on Purim is to stage a play, skit, or presentation of some kind, often referred to by its Yiddish term *spiel* (pronounced "shpeel") or *Purimspiel*. Remember that one of the encompassing themes of Purim is celebrating the fact that the Jewish people were not the victims in the story. We turned the tables on our enemies and were victorious. Therefore, most of the routines that we take for granted in the synagogue are turned around as well. Instead of sitting quietly and wearing clothes appropriate for temple, we turn the sanctuary into something resembling a festive costume party. And in place of the rabbi and cantor leading services in a staid, serious manner (although clearly you've never been to *my* shul), members of the congregation come up and poke fun at everyone and everything through scenes, songs, and parodies.

Jewish suffering? Not on Purim.

At Home

As on most of the other Jewish holidays, you need not be religious, belong to a temple, or even set foot in a sanctuary to appreciate and take part in the holiday of Purim. While there are certain aspects of this

THERE ARE many varieties of *Purimspiels* out there, ranging from a few people getting up to act out a little skit to individuals or small groups performing original song parodies, all the way to professional-quality staged productions. Some synagogues (usually larger ones with generous budgets) plan for this event all year and present incredible shows.

There's no single, correct way for any temple to present a *spiel*, nor is there even a requirement for there to be one at all. It's yet another tradition that helps show that on this one day in the Jewish calendar we're not taking ourselves too seriously.

festival that are clearly meant to be enjoyed in large groups (try putting on a *Purimspiel* while you're sitting on your couch in sweatpants), you can recognize and participate in Purim in any venue you choose.

Know Your Enemy

One of the most important lessons that we learn from Purim is to never forget . . . I mean, remember to blot out . . . that is, remember and then forget that we remembered all the while keeping the memory alive of the tribe of Amalek, the archetype of the anti-Semite throughout history. Amalek makes sense more as an idea rather than as one group of ancient tribesmen.

Certainly, there have been many Amaleks throughout Jewish history. One need not comb through pages of obscure Jewish history books to find examples. Think Hitler. Saddam Hussein. Ahmadinejad. I don't think that it's any accident that two episodes of Jewish history that couldn't feel more different from each other—the story of Purim and remembering the Holocaust—both teach us to "never forget."

Many Jews around the world are incredibly fortunate to live in a time and place where they don't routinely fear anti-Semitism. They don't live as victims or rely on their government to tolerate their existence and protect them from their neighbors. You don't need to go too far back to find a time when things weren't like that. But Purim, with its theme of remembering Amalek, teaches us to be cognizant of the existence of the anti-Semite and to realize that each generation might give rise to a modern-day Haman if we forget.

Sweet Charity

In addition to exchanging gifts of food, we are also told to give donations to the poor. Because so much of the holiday revolves around dressing up, celebrating, and acting out, it's easy for this very important *mitzvah*, or commandment, to be overlooked. Furthermore, Jews are always commanded to give *tzedakah*, charity. It's incorporated into our mission statement of *tikkun olam*—that is, repairing the world and making it a better place. There's never a time when we're *not* obligated to give *tzedakah*. Still, we should make a special effort on Purim to donate to those in need. There's never a shortage of worthy causes. A synagogue might have a dedicated fund that they encourage congregants to assist during Purim. Otherwise, this is a wonderful opportunity for individual families to decide on organizations or recipients that they feel are deserving.

Let's Eat
....

It wouldn't be much of a Jewish holiday if we didn't talk about eating. There happen to be a bunch of traditions and rituals associated with Purim that revolve around food. In the conclusion of the book of Esther, we read that for all time, the commemoration of Purim is to include exchanging gifts of food. This is the basis for an important custom on Purim called *mishloach manot* (in Hebrew) or *shaloch manos* (in Yiddish). Both terms mean the same thing—sending portions of food—and are interchangeable.

Because the word that appears in the original text is plural (*manot*, or "portions"), it is traditional to choose at least two different kinds of food and present them to someone else. Often temples will have a formal *mishloach manot* program so that for a nominal fee you can send other members of the congregation a small food basket in your name. But this is something that is easily done by just giving food to someone else. For instance, when you go to work sometime around Purim, bring donuts and coffee for everyone. You'll be everyone's favorite around the office *and* you will have fulfilled an important Purim *mitzvah*. Talk about win-win.

It's also traditional on Purim to have a big meal or feast. (That box of donuts you ended up eating doesn't count.) There's nothing else that's required; you don't have to know any special prayers or incorporate certain rituals. You just have to eat!

Finally, there is one dessert item that has become a traditional staple of Purim—*hamantashen* (the plural form of *hamantash*, which is much less commonly used). Like lots of other customs that have been passed through the generations, there's a bunch of different stories about where *hamantashen* came from. *Hamantashen* are triangular-shaped pastries with a filling of some sort in the middle—often fruit, poppy, or sometimes prune. Anyone under the age of 143 will usually prefer the fruit ones. The word is sometimes translated as "Haman's pockets" or "Haman's ears," which I suppose means something like "we've beat him, let's eat him."

The probable explanation is a little more prosaic. Most likely, *hamantashen* started out as simply pastry filled with poppy—in Yiddish, *mun*. So if someone accurately referred to this treat as a poppy-pocket, in Yiddish that would be something like *muntashen*. Somewhere along the line, someone added one syllable to this venerable treat so that first part sounded more like "Haman," and boom! You now have your traditional Purim food.

The Bottom Line

Purim is what's known as a minor festival. It is not mentioned in the Torah, since all the action is recorded in the much later Writings section of the Bible. Even among observant Jews, there is no prohibition against work or school. It's really a little gem of a holiday. It takes a wonderful, entertaining story, infuses it with serious themes and rituals, and still directs everyone to let their hair down, celebrate, maybe have a couple drinks, and just enjoy.

CHAPTER 7

PASSOVER

BRING ON THE MATZAH

IT'S HARD to imagine a more labor-intensive holiday than
Passover. It's ironic that the festival that recognizes the Israelites'
release from bondage and slavery in Egypt actually requires the
most amount of work and preparation of any Jewish holiday during the year. Wouldn't it have made more sense to commemorate our
freedom by commanding everyone to lie on the beach for a week? No
such luck.

For some, the full extent of their Passover observance is attendance at a seder. Indeed, along with fasting on Yom Kippur and lighting Chanukah candles, these are the most common and universally
observed rituals among all Jews. But Passover, known in Hebrew as
Pesach, also includes numerous symbols and rituals, as well as a distinct set of dietary restrictions that Jews are ordered to adhere to for
the duration of the holiday.

Just like Sukkot back in chapter 3, Passover is one of the Three Pilgrimage Festivals. Jews in ancient times would make a pilgrimage to the Temple in Jerusalem for this holiday in order to offer animal sacrifices. They appreciated getting a lot of exercise along the way because of all the matzah they were eating. Let's start looking closely at where Passover came from and how we observe its many rituals.

The Back Story

Maybe I should just wait here while you go watch *The Ten Commandments*. I think it nicely sums up everything you need to know. On second thought, I'll save us both some time. Who can sit through all but the last fifteen minutes of that movie, anyway?

Unlike a lot of the other holidays that are mandated in the Torah, we get more than a passing set of directions for Passover. To be sure, much of the Torah itself could be considered part of the Passover story. We have the story of Joseph and his brothers at the end of the book of Genesis. The conclusion of that story places the Israelites in Egypt and sets up all the action that follows in Exodus.

We open the book of Exodus, and the actual story of Passover, with the introduction of a new Pharaoh, one who, we are told, "knew not Joseph." Already, we know we're in trouble with this new ruler. Taken literally, it's improbable that any Pharaoh, even three hundred or so years later, would not have any knowledge of Joseph. To the Egyptians, Joseph was a kind of savior in his time. He singlehandedly saved the entire kingdom when famine was ravaging the whole land. He was the viceroy of Egypt, the then-Pharaoh's own right-hand man. For a subsequent ruler of Egypt to come along and not know about Joseph would be akin to future American leaders not having any knowledge of Benjamin Franklin. It doesn't pass the common-sense test.

Instead, let's interpret the statement that he "knew not Joseph" another way. Perhaps he *chose* not to know about Joseph. In many ways, Pharaoh might be considered the very first anti-Semite. He hated the Israelites for no apparent reason other than the fact that they were Israelites. He even tried to erase any positive accomplishments of the past by denying the importance of Joseph and what he did to save Egypt.

For some reason, this Pharaoh views the Israelites living in his land as the enemy and an imminent threat. He sees how numerous they are and believes that they could multiply even further and eventually ally with his enemies and rise up against him and Egypt. Pharaoh proceeds to do two things. First, he enslaves all the Israelites, requiring them to toil under extremely harsh conditions. Next, he makes a crude attempt at population control by ordering that all male Israelite babies be killed immediately by being thrown into the Nile River. The baby girls will be allowed to live. Pharaoh figures that between these two decisive acts, he'll be able to keep the burgeoning Israelite population in check. This serves as the backdrop for the birth of Moses.

IN DEPTH

ONE OFTEN-MISSED but fascinating detail in this story is the mention of two Egyptian midwives, Shifrah and Puah. Even though they were Egyptian, we are told that they feared God and refused to go along with Pharaoh's decree to drown the male babies. Word reached the royal throne, and they were summoned to answer for their actions before Pharoah.

Just stop and imagine that! Two lowly female midwives were ordered to stand before the mightiest ruler of the land, one whom most Egyptians treated as a god in his own right. And these two women had the presence of mind to not only defend their actions but also come up with a plausible lie in front of Pharaoh. They told him, "It's not our fault that the male babies are surviving. The Israelite women give birth so quickly that we don't have time to even get there to deliver the babies."

Shifrah and Puah are Jewish history's first examples of righteous Gentiles. We read in this story that, because of their brave and moral behavior, God rewarded them by providing them with substantial households.

The story of Moses's birth and survival is iconic. His mother, Yocheved, is able to avoid detection and hide her labor because she gives birth early. She takes her male baby to the river, puts him in a floating basket, and sends him down the Nile to safety. Moses's big sister, Miriam, is tasked with keeping a careful eye on the basket and reporting back on what happens.

Sure enough, the basket makes its way to where Pharaoh's daughter is hanging out with her servants. She finds the basket and opens it to discover that there's a baby inside! Delighted, she decides to keep it as her own. She gives the boy the name of *Moshe*, based on the Hebrew phrase "drawing him out," with "of the water" being implied. (Apparently Pharaoh's daughter spoke Hebrew.)

Moses is raised as a prince in Pharaoh's household and he lives a life of royal privilege, even though it's known that he's really a Hebrew. That all changes on one fateful day when he is out among the Hebrew slaves and comes across an Egyptian taskmaster beating a slave. This proves to be too much for him to bear, and, after looking around to see if anyone is watching, he strikes the taskmaster, killing him. Moses attempts to conceal his actions by burying the Egyptian in a shallow grave in the sand.

Soon after, he is again out among the slaves and sees two Israelites quarreling with each other. Moses tries to help, but his intervention is not appreciated. One of the slaves confronts him and asks, "Who put you in charge around here? Are you going to kill me like you killed that Egyptian?"

IN DEPTH

WHERE DID the familiar name *Moses* come from? It doesn't even sound like *Moshe*.

It appears for the first time in the Greek translation of the Bible, also known as the Septuagint. The letter *S* was added to the name because, in Greek, a male name cannot end with a vowel. So *Moshe* became *Mose*, which eventually was written as *Moses*.

One thing that goes unmentioned in this story is why the Hebrews reacted so negatively toward Moses. After all, he was a Hebrew himself. He came to the rescue of a slave being beaten and took action to stop his oppression. Then he tried to make peace between two arguing slaves. It's a mystery as to why he was resented by the others. Perhaps the slaves were unable to discern between this Hebrew in a position of power and their Egyptian oppressors.

In any case, Moses realizes that if these two slaves know about his crime, then others probably do as well. Undoubtedly Pharaoh himself will find out. Moses makes his escape and runs away to the wilderness of Midian. There he comes across seven attractive women drawing water from a well. Their father likes the way Moses comes across and offers him his oldest daughter, Tzipporah (thanks, Dad). They marry and have a couple of sons. Then things get really strange.

One day Moses is out tending the sheep and sees what eventually becomes the most famous shrubbery in human history. He observes a bush that is on fire but not being consumed by the flames. As he approaches it warily, he hears a voice emanate from the bush. "I am God," says the voice. "I know that my people are suffering. Go to Pharaoh and tell him that I order him to let the Israelites go free."

What would you do in this situation? Tell the bush that you'll do it? Look for the hidden speaker and camera? Get the hedge clippers? Moses does something rather human in this otherwise surreal situation. He starts to argue with the voice in the burning bush. First he asks, "Who am *I*, that I should go to mighty Pharaoh and tell him to do this?" Then he wonders, "Why in the world would Pharaoh believe *me*?" These are the reasonable doubts of a reluctant prophet.

God gives Moses a couple of magic tricks with which to impress Pharaoh. He tells Moses that he will be able to turn his rod into a serpent (and back into a rod) and to transform a cup into blood into water. Moses still argues, and he delivers to God his famous line, "I am slow of speech and slow of tongue."

At this point, God gets angry with Moses! Apparently the ruler of the universe is not used to having His orders questioned. God finally instructs Moses to take his older brother, Aaron, along with him to be his spokesman. Together they enter the royal court to speak with Pharaoh.

IN DEPTH

WHAT EXACTLY does it mean that Moses is "slow of speech and slow of tongue"? We are not explicitly told in the Torah, but there is a story in the Midrash that gives us the background information. Written by the rabbis generations after the words of the Torah, Midrashic texts exist to provide extra information about what's in the Torah, often by giving us additional episodes. The Midrash can be compared to the bonus material you get when you buy a DVD. Its stories are like the deleted scenes that never made it into the movie.

According to this Midrash, Pharaoh was warned by his astrologers that a male Hebrew would eventually rise up and overthrow him. Yet Pharaoh's own daughter had adopted a Hebrew baby, and everyone in the palace had become fond of him. Pharaoh's advisors urged him to kill the baby, but he resisted. Finally they came up with the idea of a test. They placed two plates in front of baby Moses—one filled with shiny, sparkling gems, and the other full of hot, burning coals. If the baby reached for the gems, then he would be considered cunning enough to represent a future threat and should be killed.

Obviously, any baby would be more attracted to something shiny, and baby Moses started reaching for the jewelry. Just then, an invisible angel took Moses's arm and moved it over to the hot coals. He picked up the burning coals and, as babies are known to do, he put the coals in his mouth, burning his lips and tongue. Pharaoh and his advisors assumed they had a not-so-bright baby on their hands and no longer considered him a threat. From then on, Moses had a significant speech impediment (and a fear of barbeque).

Moses's and Aaron's initial meeting with Pharaoh does not go well. Had they really been expecting him to say "Sure!" when they announced that God wanted the Israelites freed? Moses tries to wow Pharoah with his two little parlor tricks, but Pharaoh's own magicians are able to duplicate them exactly, so Pharaoh is unimpressed.

Moses threatens Pharaoh with a series of plagues that God will rain upon him and the Egyptians if he doesn't comply with God's order. After each of the famous plagues, we read that Pharaoh's heart is hardened, and he refuses to free the Israelites. This takes some explanation. After each of the first five plagues, the same thing happens. Pharaoh cries "Uncle!" and begs Moses to make it stop. He promises to let the Israelites go, having seen the error of his ways and the power of God. Then, when life is back to normal, Pharaoh has a change of heart and refuses, leading to the next plague.

But after plague number six, something different happens. We read that God hardens Pharaoh's heart—almost as if Pharaoh's own decision-making process is taken out of the equation. In this case, is it really Pharaoh's fault that he refuses God's command? Is it fair to punish him and the Egyptians with more plagues?

Some commentaries have explained that because Pharaoh was such a bad apple, he deserved whatever punishment he got. Furthermore, this was God's opportunity to demonstrate His power and divine might to the rest of Egypt as well as the Israelites, who probably weren't following events too closely due to their unbearable workload. Perhaps a more likely explanation is the assumption that Pharaoh would never have let the slaves go under any circumstances. So the text skips the unnecessary part where Pharaoh first relents and then reneges.

Finally we get to the last plague—the slaying of the first-born. This, you may notice, parallels Pharaoh's earlier decree that all male Hebrew children should be killed. The Israelites are told to take the blood of a lamb and smear it on their doorposts. The angel of death will see that blood and *pass over* those houses. In all other houses, the first-born child will die (including cattle, by the way). Even Pharaoh is not exempt, and his own heir is killed.

Now Pharaoh is a broken king. Defeated, he tells Moses, "Go. Get lost. Take everyone. Just get out." Moses is only too happy

IN DEPTH

THERE'S A motif running through this story that is easily missed by the average reader. Throughout the action, God is actually mocking Pharaoh. The Egyptians, along with Pharaoh himself, consider Pharaoh to be a god deserving of worship. Then the real God (capital *G*) comes along to paint a different picture.

While it may sound like an extraordinary feat of magic to turn a rod into a serpent or water into blood, these were like ancient versions of pulling a rabbit from your hat or pretending to take a quarter out of a kid's ear. It might be compared to appearing before the most powerful and intimidating monarch in the world and telling him you have divine powers. Then you take two interlocking metal rings, wave a magic wand, and somehow pull them apart. You'd be laughed out of there (and maybe locked up for your trouble). This is the same thing. Here, God is purposely wasting Pharaoh's time with magical nonsense so Pharaoh won't take anything seriously. This sets up the action to follow.

Later, when God punishes Egypt with the famous plagues, many of them serve to mock Pharaoh as well. Frogs? It's God's most slapstick plague. Others, like turning the Nile into blood, afflicting cattle with diseases, and even killing all the first-born Egyptian children, take sacred Egyptian icons and demonstrate how weak and powerless they are.

to comply, but he feels that Pharaoh could change his mind any minute. So he orders the Israelites to hurry, get packed up, and get going.

In what later becomes the most famed incident of culinary mismanagement ever, the Israelite women don't have time to let their bread rise. They take the flat, unrisen dough and bring that with them instead. Imagine how all of our lives would have been radically different if only they could have waited another half hour. But it turns out that Moses is smart to hurry everyone along. Pharaoh has one more incredible change of heart. He looks around his now-empty kingdom and wonders what in the world he was thinking, letting all of his slaves go. Immediately, he gathers up his mighty army and orders them to pursue the Israelites and bring them back.

By now, the Israelites have made it to the edge of the Red Sea, and in the distance they see the formidable Egyptian army coming after them. You can imagine why the Israelites would have been frightened and doubtful of Moses. Not that long before, they had been toiling as slaves, perhaps unaware of the drama that was playing out with Moses, Pharaoh, and God. Then suddenly a leader comes to them, announces that they're free to go, and leads them into the wilderness where they are pursued by an army. Of course they would question Moses and cry out in fear.

In a bitingly sarcastic line, they ask Moses, "What, there weren't enough graves in Egypt, so you had to bring us out here to be killed?"

Moses tells them to stop worrying and watch. He takes his staff and stretches it out over the sea. In history's first example of special effects, the sea parts right down the middle, leaving a path of dry land. Meanwhile, God makes sure the pursuing Egyptian army is held at bay by producing a pillar of fire between them and the Israelites. (Note to Egyptians: You might have considered *this* a good time to rethink your mission.)

Moses leads the Israelites across the dry sea-bed to the other side. Once the Israelites reach the opposite shore, God removes the pillar of fire and the Egyptians continue their ill-fated pursuit. We all know what happens next. As the Egyptians are in the middle of the parted waters, God pulls the plug on the miracle and the sea comes crashing down on every soldier, horse, and chariot. No one is left except a stunned Pharaoh, watching helplessly from the other side. The Israelites sing a song of praise to God, and its well-known Hebrew text—*Mi Chamocha*—is recited in contemporary synagogue services every day of the year.

Because of this epic story of God's might, the Torah commands us to observe this festival of Pesach for seven days. By now, you're already familiar with the extra day that is celebrated outside of Israel, just like we saw for many of the other Jewish holidays, so we celebrate Passover for eight days.

Leaven-Worth

Passover comes with its own complicated set of directions for keeping kosher. Jews who strictly adhere to *kashrut* (the Jewish dietary laws) throughout the year need to add many more rules to their observance for the week of Passover. Let's go over the basics.

In the Torah, we are instructed to commemorate the Israelites' hurried escape from Egypt and the fact that they did not have time for their bread to rise by ridding our homes, cupboards, pantries, cars, desks, pockets, and any other places of all *chametz*—that is, leavened foods.

All grains can become leavened unless the process is prevented under strict supervision. For instance, the most famous unleavened food of all, matzah, is simply made from flour and water, and then baked. However, the rabbis determined (perhaps after watching the Ancient Food Network) that after eighteen minutes the grain will become leavened, so all kosher-for-Passover matzah is baked no more than eighteen minutes after the flour and water are mixed. In fact, all Passover foods are watched this closely during production to make sure that not one iota of leavening is introduced into the mix. That's why perfectly good kosher food, even traditional Passover staples such as matzah or wine, must be specially marked "Kosher for Passover" on the label, indicating that they have undergone this increased level of scrutiny.

This becomes something of a challenge for an observant Jewish household. Picture your kitchen with all its drawers and cupboards, cooking and cutting surfaces, and corners along the floor and the shelves. Traditionally, observant Jews set out to make the kitchen, and in fact the entire house, completely free of *chametz* before Passover begins. That entails a comprehensive and exhaustive cleaning of every last inch of the kitchen. Not even a crumb should be missed.

Usually every surface, including the inside of the refrigerator, drawers, and cabinets, is covered with some kind of liner so that Passover foods won't come in contact with remnants of the foods that aren't kosher for Passover. In kosher homes, two sets of dishes are typically used, one set for dairy foods and another for meals with meat. On Passover, you bring out two *more* sets of dishes that are used only during Passover, one set for dairy and one for meat, as well as utensils, cutlery, and pots and pans. Traditionally, one would never use dishes that routinely touch *chametz* to hold Passover foods. As you can imagine, it becomes a challenge to find space for everything. Often that means boxing up and putting away the year-round stuff to make room for these once-a-year dishes.

Search and Ye Shall Find (A Whole Section Perfect for Families)

It's almost impossible to rid your home of *every* bit of *chametz*, even for the most thorough cleaner. Might there be one corner that someone forgot? Could there be a piece of cracker or even a *crumb* hiding in some forgotten cranny of the kitchen? Of course.

We've got you covered. There are a couple of rituals that now follow the exhaustive cleaning. The first is "searching for *chametz*," and it's particularly fun for the entire family, assuming anyone is still talking to each other after all that hard work.

During the Big Clean, it's customary to take a few little pieces of *chametz*, maybe a few crackers or little pieces of bread, and put them aside. Then, after it gets dark on the evening before Passover begins, the family symbolically searches for those last bits of *chametz*. Picture a religious game of hide-and-seek. Traditionally, this process is done using a candle, a wooden spoon, and a feather. Really. It sounds like some hazing incident from a three-thousand-year-old frat party.

Someone will take the pieces of *chametz* and place them strategically throughout the house, or maybe in just one room. With the lights off, everyone else (perfect for kids) will walk through the house (or room) holding a lit candle (or, if that sounds like an accident waiting to happen, a flashlight will be fine) looking for the concealed *chametz*. When each piece is found, the searcher takes the feather and brushes the piece onto the wooden spoon. Then the piece is emptied into a paper or plastic bag. That is repeated until all the hidden *chametz* is found and removed. The feather, wooden spoon, and candle (make sure to blow it out first) are placed in the bag along with those last pieces of *chametz*, and the whole thing is put aside for the next morning. If you used a flashlight instead of a candle for safety reasons, feel free to just put it back in your drawer.

Burn, Bread, Burn!

When you wake up the next morning and see a bag filled with stale pieces of bread, a candle, a wooden spoon, and a feather, you might be wondering what in the world you did last night and whether anyone got hurt. Then you remember that you performed the ritual act of searching for *chametz*, and now it's time to finish the job.

You take the entire bag and burn it. How you actually do that is up to you. You could find a large metal container and put the bag inside. Some people will take it all outside for an added measure of safety and to prevent their smoke detectors from going off. In religious communities, there are sometimes giant communal bonfires where residents can bring their *chametz* to be destroyed.

After the *chametz* is burned, a text in Aramaic is recited. We've seen this before, most notably on Yom Kippur with the Kol Nidrei prayer—whenever Aramaic rather than Hebrew is used, it reminds us that a text or ritual was so widely observed or treasured by the people that the original language was preserved. Remember that in ancient times, Aramaic was analogous to today's English. It was the common, everyday spoken language, whereas Hebrew was reserved only for prayer and holy texts.

This Aramaic text states that all *chametz* that may still inadvertently remain in a person's household is considered to be gone, destroyed, kaput, and hereby nonexistent. The small sample that is being burned symbolizes the fact that no more *chametz* can be found in a person's possession. It acknowledges the fact that it's not humanly possible to eradicate every single crumb, even with a thorough cleaning, so anything that might accidentally have been overlooked is now considered dust.

Bread for Sale

Not only are Jews supposed to do this rigorous level of spring cleaning to rid their homes of any traces of *chametz*, but we are also forbidden from seeing it, benefiting from it, or even *owning* it. How is that possible?

Imagine spending a hard day of work cleaning the kitchen, boxing up and removing dishes and non-Passover foods, and lining shelves. All of the year-round food is taken away and maybe put in another location, perhaps in the basement, or in some otherwise unused pantry. What about the perishables? You can't exactly take stuff out of the fridge, box it up, and then replace it after eight days.

The rabbis of old came up with a loophole. Since we are not allowed to own any *chametz*, we'll just sell it to someone. And because this law applies to all Jews, we require the services of a non-Jew to fulfill this requirement. You enter into an agreement with a non-Jewish person who agrees to buy all of the *chametz* currently in your possession. To make it a real transaction, money should change hands, even if it's only a dollar. The sale, of course, is only symbolic and serves to fulfill the instruction to not own any *chametz* during Passover. According to the arrangement, the ownership of the *chametz* reverts back after the festival is over.

In many synagogues, it's very easy to perform this process. A congregant will fill out a form (printed and distributed ahead of time) appointing the rabbi as his "agent" to sell the *chametz* for him. Then the rabbi finds one non-Jewish person (more often than not the temple custodian, who is happy to go along in mystified cooperation) and arranges for him to take ownership of the entire congregation's *chametz*. Luckily he doesn't have to find a storage facility for everyone's groceries. Everyone's *chametz* stays where it is, out of sight and out of mind for the duration of the festival. According to Jewish law, they simply don't own it anymore.

Reality Bites

Reading all this, you may have become completely overwhelmed pages ago. For those who are used to this level of observance, this process of cleaning, shopping for new food, moving, boxing, disposing, and yes, burning is a challenging but expected activity every year. Even for people who love Passover, it's a lot of hard work.

But what about those who are unfamiliar with these rituals and are looking to incorporate some level of traditional observance into their lives? How about an average Jewish family that didn't grow up with a lot of this but has learned that Passover is an important Jewish holiday?

While these Passover observances may sound like a huge obstacle to all but the most committed and intense group of people, you can actually get started easily. You can include elements of these rituals within your own family, and then as these elements become routine, it's easy to start doing more if you want.

Some Jews who otherwise don't keep kosher throughout the year will make an effort to avoid bread for the week of Passover. Some restaurants will even make matzah available for their customers who won't eat bread. Some households that don't keep kosher at all during the year will still pull out another set or two of dishes for Passover. Others might use year-round plates but not serve bread. There is a lot of room for variations of personal observance, all while remembering the festival and keeping its traditions and rituals in mind.

Order! Order!

The most recognizable and celebrated ritual of Passover is the seder. The word *seder* means "order." This signifies that everything we do is to be done in a specific order. Otherwise, we might decide to eat first and then get around to reciting some of the blessings, or we might sing some fun songs at the start of the meal that usually appear at the end. The seder comes in its prescribed order for a reason—we're supposed to immerse ourselves from beginning to end in the story of the Israelites' slavery and then freedom from bondage. The seder tells a story that we in turn are supposed to teach our children.

During the seder, we read from a special book that is used only for this specific occasion—the *Hagaddah*. In recent years, there have been various *Hagaddot* (the plural form) that focus on a specific theme or special interest. For instance, one *Hagaddah* may be targeted toward families with young children, so that there are more illustrations and the translations are simplified. Another example is a feminist *Hagaddah*, which might include readings about the female characters involved in the Exodus from Egypt. No matter how many varieties of *Hagaddot* exist, they'll all have the basic order of the seder in common.

While I don't have space here to analyze in detail every aspect of the Passover meal, I'll highlight some of the most basic symbols of the seder and discuss the important elements. This will lay out the fundamentals for the person preparing a seder for the first time or for the seder attendee who is somewhat unsure of what to expect.

Plate of Symbols

When setting the table for the seder, you put a special plate, called (predictably enough) the seder plate, in the middle of the table. The seder plate holds five important foods.

- *Karpas*: This refers to a green vegetable, symbolizing that Passover is the Festival of Spring. The vegetables used most often are parsley or celery, but you can use anything green. At a traditional seder, the *karpas* is eaten early on, and then there's a long time before the actual dinner is served. This can become dicey for antsy kids and bored relatives and friends who showed up for the huge dinner and realized they got more than they bargained for. After eating *karpas*, feel free to put out plates of more *karpas*-type hors d'oeuvres. You can put out celery and carrot sticks, or maybe slices of potato for people to snack on while they're waiting for the main course.
- *Charoset*: There are probably as many different recipes for charoset as there are seats at the table. It's a mixture that includes nuts, wine, apples, and cinnamon. Charoset reminds us of the mortar used by the slaves. Fortunately, it tastes better than that.
- *Zero'ah* (shank bone): This is the only meat item on the seder plate. We put the shank bone of a lamb on the plate to remind us of the Passover sacrifice that was required in Temple times. We don't eat it; it's just for looking. It also reminds us of Moses telling the Israelites to slaughter a lamb and smear its blood on the doorposts of their homes so the angel of death would pass over their houses.
- *Beitzah* (roasted egg): This is another reminder of the Temple and its destruction. Eggs were a food often eaten by mourners, so we include one on the seder plate to show that we grieve over the destruction of the Temple. In addition, eggs were often considered fertility symbols, and because Passover is a holiday of spring and continuity, it's natural that we might include some aspect of renewal.
- *Maror* (bitter herbs): This is one of the two foods, along with matzah, that we are specifically instructed to eat during the Passover seder. It reminds us of the bitterness that the Israelite slaves felt

during their years of suffering. People usually use horseradish for *maror*, but it can be any vegetable that has a bitter taste.

Does Anyone Have Any Questions?

Remember that the main objective of the seder is to tell a story. One of the most effective methods of instructing is to involve the student in the question-and-answer process, rather than just sitting the person down and lecturing for a couple of hours. So toward the beginning of the seder, we open up the *Hagaddah* and recite the Four Questions.

Traditionally, the Four Questions are asked by the youngest person in attendance, because presumably this would be the individual likely to have the most questions and to have the greatest need of information. There are generations of Jews who remember the abject fear they felt when they were called upon as young kids to stand up in front of everyone present and sing their way through the Four Questions. There's actually no requirement as to who must recite the questions, and you can have any kid or adult, individually or together, ask them.

Let's look at the actual text of the Four Questions and see how it sets the tone for what's important during the seder. We begin by asking one general and all-encompassing question: *Why is this night different from all other nights?* Then four more specific questions follow.

1. On all other nights, we eat both leavened and non-leavened foods. (Translation: Throughout the year we eat bread and regular stuff, and we can also have matzah too, but I don't know why you'd want to if you didn't have to.) *Why do we only eat matzah tonight?*
2. On all other nights, we eat all kinds of vegetables and herbs. *Why do we eat bitter herbs (maror) tonight?*
3. On all other nights, we don't dip our foods. *Why do we dip our foods twice tonight?*
4. On all other nights, we can sit at dinner however we want (until Mom yells at us to sit up straight). *Why do we recline tonight?*

My guess is that most people familiar with Passover are fairly comfortable with the first two questions and then are somewhat mystified by numbers 3 and 4. It's interesting to note that after posing the questions, the *Hagaddah* does not simply launch into the answers. I suspect that if the Four Questions were followed immediately with the Four Answers, most seders would run about ten minutes long. Instead, these are almost like discussion questions, meant to pique the interest of those in attendance, especially children who are eager to learn the story.

Fear not—together we'll go through the answers and find out what they tell us about the seder and the Passover story.

Why Do We Only Eat Matzah Tonight?

This one's easy, and you already know it. We eat matzah because the Israelites rushed out of Egypt before their bread had time to rise.

Why Do We Eat Bitter Herbs (Maror) Tonight?

What exactly is a bitter herb? Well, it can be any vegetable that's bitter. In many households, we fulfill the requirement to eat a bitter herb by eating horseradish. In fact, this has become so popular that

IN DEPTH

THERE ARE usually hidden messages written into the holidays that we observe. For instance, Sukkot teaches us about the fragility of life. Rosh Hashanah and Yom Kippur stress the theme of life and death. Chanukah helps teach us about the balance between religious pride and assimilation.

On Passover, the traditional food is also food for thought. *Chametz*, food that is leavened and rises, symbolizes our own inflated sense of ourselves. We might begin to think that we're the most important people around, perhaps even more essential than God. Matzah, which by definition is a flat, simple, and often bland food, tells us the opposite. No matter how much we may go through our lives seeking self-aggrandizement, there's always something more important in our lives.

horseradish has transformed itself into something of a classic ethnic Jewish food. On almost every Jewish holiday, not just Passover, you can walk into a supermarket and find it on sale. Grocery store managers must think that whenever Jews gather, they consume gallons of horseradish.

In Hebrew, the bitter herb is called *maror*. The Torah tells us in a couple of places to eat *maror* in order to remember how the Egyptians made our ancestors' lives bitter. Consider what an effective way that is to remember something. We could just try to remember the bitterness and suffering that the Israelites experienced, or we could include a food that tastes bitter (and too much of which literally brings tears to the eyes) to make that emotion all the more powerful.

A lot of people use the prepared horseradish found on the store shelf. Red horseradish simply has beets mixed in to give it some color and take a little bit of the potency away; white horseradish is usually stronger. Any Jewish grandmother will tell you that back in her day, no one would have been caught dead using store-bought horseradish. You made your own, by grinding the raw horseradish root (and the skin of your knuckles), and you had tears running down your face the whole time from the fumes. And don't even talk about food processors. Feh!

Note that there's no biblical or other requirement to use horseradish. Some people might take a piece of romaine lettuce or endive, for instance, which are bitter-tasting vegetables. But it's not as much fun as watching your eight-year-old cousin put way too much horseradish in his mouth and seeing his face turn bright red. Priceless.

Why Do We Dip Our Foods Twice Tonight?

This is a little more challenging. Many Jews can identify one time during the seder when we dip one food into the other, but two times?

Let's take one dip at a time. Soon after the Four Questions are recited, we come to *karpas*. As noted before, this refers to a green vegetable, reminiscent of the spring. However, we don't just grab a piece of parsley and eat it. Instead, we take the vegetable and dip it into salt water. The water represents the tears of the Israelite slaves.

The second time we combine foods like this is later in the seder, just before dinner is served. When it's time to take some *maror*, we first dip it into some *charoset* before eating it. This may have come about to lessen the bitter taste of the *maror*, or possibly to add to the feeling of bitterness by using the slaves' mortar as well.

The seder itself is somewhat of a snapshot in time. Its format hearkens back to Hellenistic times, when the ancient Greeks would hold huge feasts and symposia. One of the common customs in those times was to dip different foods into one another before eating. (Table manners have changed somewhat since then.) It's no accident that such food dipping is featured so prominently in the seder. Another characteristic of those times leads us to . . .

Why Do We Recline Tonight?

Can't you imagine attending a huge Greek feast, resting on one elbow, with servants feeding you grapes from the vine? That image is not too far off from explaining why we recline at a seder. Again, this tradition is modeled on Greek symposia. Those present at the table probably lay on reclining couches instead of straight-backed chairs.

During the rest of the year, we would never think of leaning or reclining at the dinner table. At the Passover seder, however, we are supposed to recline a little while sitting. This symbolizes the fact that we are now a free people, able to relax and take our time at the meal. Slaves could never have done that. They would have to eat fast, probably while standing, and grab whatever was available.

Today, it's customary to recline a bit to the left while sitting at the seder table. While it may be a bit awkward to maintain that posture for the entire time, you should at least lean a little bit while you drink the four cups of wine (that gets easier with each cup) and eat the matzah and *maror* after the blessings. Sometimes people will be seated with small pillows to make it easier to lean back, and to further illustrate the theme of freedom.

Why do we recline to the left? Does it matter? Consider this a ritual example of form following function. Leaning to the right was once believed to produce a choking hazard, because the ancient rabbis thought that food could end up heading down your windpipe instead of your esophagus. Perhaps there were a lot of Jews who reclined to the right, but we haven't heard much from that group.

Care for Some Wine?

One of the basic components of the seder is the four cups of wine. Throughout history, how many kids have secretly gotten drunk on Manishewitz right under the unknowing eyes of their parents, aunts, uncles, and grandparents?

Throughout the seder, we recite the blessing over wine four times. The most common reason given for this is because God used four different synonymous verbs in one passage from Exodus to describe how He would rescue the Israelites from slavery. Each cup of wine, then, parallels one of those important phrases of redemption. Of course, wine itself is also a common and powerful symbol of joy, which is why it's included at all Jewish life-cycle events and other happy occasions.

It's not necessary to down four full glasses of wine during the seder. As always, grape juice can always be substituted, and in any case, you don't have to finish what's in the cup.

Teach Your Children Well

We come across the theme of "four" again in the section of the *Hagaddah* that now describes four imaginary sons. Other than the fact that the ancient rabbis must have considered it unthinkable that a girl might actually want to learn about Passover, I find these four kinds of students to be amazingly accurate. In fact, rather than identifying them as four sons, or even four children, I would go further and say that this passage simply describes four types of people in general. I have come across all of them many times when teaching both kids and adults throughout the year. So when the *Hagaddah* uses the word "son," we can substitute "child" or even "person."

Let's take a look at what the *Hagaddah* describes.

The Wise Child

We've come across this kind of kid often. He already knows a lot of the information. He's smart, enthusiastic, and eager to learn more, so he asks you to explain more about Passover. But what can you teach him that he doesn't already know? The *Hagaddah* tells us to delve deeper into the Passover laws and customs, from beginning to end.

PERFECT FOR FAMILIES

IN ADDITION to the prescribed four cups of wine, there's also a fifth cup at the seder known as Elijah's Cup. It's named after a famous prophet from the Bible who had the distinction of being one of the only biblical characters never to die. Instead, he ascended to heaven in a flaming chariot. As a result, Elijah is often considered a source of mystical characteristics. We also assume that since he never actually died, he might be available to make the occasional appearance throughout the Jewish year. We regularly invoke his name at every circumcision ceremony as well as the Havdalah service that concludes the Sabbath each week.

When the rabbis were deciding on the proper order of the seder, they couldn't settle on whether to require four or five cups of wine. The argument went back and forth without a clear resolution until, as a compromise, they decided to include the four cups that we have now and then to add a special fifth cup only for Elijah. Just after the meal is concluded during the seder, that cup is filled and Elijah is ceremonially invited into the house to enjoy the wine set aside for him.

It's common for the adults at the seder to have the kids open the door to welcome Elijah. The kids also take great pleasure in carefully examining Elijah's cup to see if the level of wine inside went down even a little.

The Wicked Child

Wow, can you imagine a teacher calling a parent at home and saying, "I'm sorry Mrs. Johnson, but I can't teach little Tommy a thing. Your kid is just wicked"? This category could well be the most misunderstood of the four. It seems to describe the exact opposite of the previous child. That kid was wise and eager, and this one is evil and ready to turn his back on everything. It's easy to picture the "wicked" child as a troubled kid who is always getting into trouble. But he is actually a lot more complicated than that.

The *Hagaddah* tells us that the wicked child asks, "What do these laws and customs mean to you?" By stressing "to you," he's saying that this is important to other people but not to him. He removes all the responsibility from himself and says that he doesn't want to be bothered with anything having to do with this tradition.

But what always goes unnoticed is that the wicked child isn't just being obnoxious. He is not simply saying, "All of this stuff is stupid and I don't want to do it." Instead, he's actually quoting from the Torah, which instructs the Israelites to ask that very question: "What do these laws and customs mean to you?" He's just being bitingly sarcastic in stressing "*to you*," as if to say, "Ha, I'm using the Torah's own words to trick you." This kid is smart and knowledgeable enough to know Torah and to be able to manipulate its words to say what he wants.

I've always considered the wicked child to represent the typical teenager. He's rebellious by nature, ready to push his parents' buttons and question their beliefs. Rather than being the child whom one wants to avoid, he's actually the most interesting and real of the bunch.

How do the rabbis say you should answer his question? Here's where it helps to understand Hebrew, because in every *Hagaddah* I've seen, the English translation leaves this part out. The rabbis tell us to smack this kid in the teeth and tell him, "God did all this for you!" What a great little window on early classroom management techniques.

The Simple Child

What exactly does "simple" mean in this context? Is it someone who's not too intelligent? Someone who comes from an unsophisticated background? We can assume that the simple child is ready to learn but just doesn't know much about Passover already. The question he asks—"What is all this?"—shows that he needs a basic level of instruction. He's a beginning student. So for him, you start with the big picture and major elements of the Passover story.

Again, I find this depiction to be realistic. There are many kids and adults who are newcomers to Judaism. They have the simplest level of knowledge and sincerely seek to add to what they know.

The Child Who Does Not Know How to Ask

In many *Hagaddah* illustrations, this child is often depicted as a baby or toddler. After all, who else couldn't even ask a question? Instead, I think that there are many adults who would fit into this category, and it has nothing to do with education or intelligence.

Pretend that you wandered onto the campus of a university and found yourself in a lecture hall. It's a bunch of doctoral students discussing advanced physics. As the terms, formulas, and theorems get thrown about, there you sit in complete bafflement. You literally cannot understand a word anyone is saying. (If there are any physicists reading this now, just go along with it.)

At the end of the hour the professor wraps things up and says, "OK, does anyone have any questions?"

Could you ask a question in this scenario? Would it even be possible for you to formulate a context where anything you asked would make sense? Or would you sit there in slack-jawed incomprehension?

There are some people for whom any discussion of Judaism is so foreign and difficult to understand that they fit into this category. The *Hagaddah* tells us not to wait for this type of child to ask a question, but instead to just dive right in and try explaining some of what's going on.

The whole point of the seder, of course, is to tell the story of the Exodus from Egypt and relive what the Israelites went through. Therefore, the rabbis of the *Hagaddah* identified these four distinct types of students—the four sons—who might be typical attendees at a seder. Each kid represents a certain personality or characteristic when asking a question about the seder, and a person looking to teach about the Passover story would have to take that into consideration. It helps us remember what the real goal of the evening is, and to be aware that we might have attendees at our seders who come from diverse backgrounds and who possess different levels of knowledge.

Just Desserts

I saved this for last because it's supposed to be the last thing eaten at the seder. It's time to talk about the *afikoman*. Countless Jews have their own stories and memories about hiding and looking for the *afikoman* and getting some money as a reward for returning it to

PERFECT FOR FAMILIES

I F WE CAN'T finish the seder without the *afikoman*, then that makes it kind of valuable, doesn't it?

In many households, it has become a tradition for any kids who are present to try to steal and hide the *afikoman* right out from under the adults. They then refuse to give it back when it's time unless they get some kind of ransom. It's never too early to teach kids about blackmail and extortion.

What then follows will depend on what specific families might be comfortable with. The kids might get some coins or a little bit of money (in some houses, a lot of money) or some other prize or reward. Because handling money on a festival is against traditional Jewish law, kids might just receive a promise of something to be delivered later. Even though it sounds like something out of *The Sopranos*, it's all kept in good fun, and it really helps keep young kids involved in the seder.

their grandfather, father, or whoever was leading the seder. In a lot of households, the *afikoman* has become one of the central highlights of the seder, especially for any kids.

So what exactly is the *afikoman* and why has it taken on mythic proportions?

Earlier in the seder, the leader took one of the three pieces of matzah that were on the table, broke it in half, and put one of those halves aside. This was to become the *afikoman*, based on a Greek word for "dessert." It also represents the Passover sacrifice that we obviously can't offer anymore. The *Hagaddah* tells us that the *afikoman* must be the last thing we eat after dinner and that the seder is not complete if we don't eat it.

You Might Need the Parental Controls

As we've seen with a number of other Jewish holidays, there's often a parallel story or book of the Bible that gets worked into the holiday's observance. Specifically, our services on each of the Three Pilgrimage Festivals include the reading of a specific book found in the Writings section of the Bible. On Sukkot (see chapter 3) we read Ecclesiastes, and on Shavuot (see chapter 8) we chant the book of Ruth. On Passover we read *Shir HaShirim* (the Song of Songs), which is unlike any other book of the Bible. The Song of Songs is basically chapter after chapter of erotic love poetry. It describes two lovers who are frolicking out in the fields talking about . . . well, pretty much what you think they're talking about. What in the world is this book doing in the Bible, and why do we read it on Passover?

The rabbis have always drawn a comparison between God's relationship with the People Israel and a marriage. Both sides profess their love and commitment to each other, promising to fulfill responsibilities and uphold a *brit*, a covenant. In fact, we regularly use the word "love" in the prayer book, most notably surrounding the well-known Shema. So the concept is not unusual. Therefore, the rabbis say, the two lovers in the Song of Songs are actually metaphors for God and Israel. A for effort.

Specifically, we read this book on Passover because of the numerous and vivid descriptions of spring found within. It serves as one more reminder that Passover is also considered the Festival of Spring. Just watch out if you see your kid sneaking around the house holding a Bible.

Dew Drop In

On Shemini Atzeret (see chapter 4), we made a giant production out of our need for rain. One of the main features of that holiday was the recitation of the Prayer for Rain. The cantor donned the white *kittel*, pulled out the fancy music, and recited this lengthy prayer for rain that would ensure our very survival for the coming year.

The parallel for Passover is not as straightforward. On this holiday, we recite *Tefillat Tal*, the Prayer for Dew. Dew? Like what we have to wipe off our windshields in the morning before we leave for work?

It makes more sense when you look at it in the context of the year's agricultural and weather cycle. The Prayer for Rain comes right at the beginning of the traditional rainy season in Israel. In the spring, however, the rainy season is over, but we still hope for the proper amount of moisture in the air. It rounds out the natural course of the year. So on the first day of Passover, we pull the *kittel* back out of the closet, cue the same set of music that we used for the Prayer for Rain, and make a big fuss with a fancy prayer including poetry infused with images of dew. It vividly reminds us of the festival's agricultural roots.

The Bottom Line

Within all the countless symbols, rules, and rituals associated with Passover, I've always felt that there were a couple key concepts buried within. During the Jewish holidays, we observe various rituals that serve to remind us that as much as we think we're in control or that humans are the most important part of creation, everything we have is really because of God. As we saw in chapter 3, this was a huge part of Sukkot. We can seek to surround ourselves with luxurious and solid surroundings throughout the year, only to spend time in a flimsy structure subject to the whim of the elements.

But on Passover, we are what we eat. We spend considerable time and energy ridding our lives of *chametz*, leavened bread that can represent an inflated sense of self. Eating only flat, unrisen matzah helps to give us a little reality check. We're not quite as important as we think we are.

Next, during the seder, we recite, "In every generation, a person is obligated to regard himself as if he, personally, made the Exodus from Egypt." That's a lot different from instructing us to remember that our ancestors made the Exodus. For the duration of this holiday, maybe even for just one short time during the seder, we consider ourselves slaves who are liberated. The miracle of the Exodus and the privileges of being free are not something that we simply acknowledge happened at one time. Rather, we celebrate our own freedom as a constant and perpetual gift.

CHAPTER 8

SHAVUOT

THE FORGOTTEN
FESTIVAL

POOR SHAVUOT. Picture this important festival, sitting on the therapy couch, explaining how during its entire life it always felt overshadowed by its two famous siblings, Passover and Sukkot.

It's true. Passover and Sukkot get all the attention and include a myriad of interesting, often-observed, and recognizable customs and rituals. Meanwhile Shavuot, a holiday that is considered equally as important, is relegated to virtual obscurity for a variety of reasons which we'll see.

Shavuot is the festival that commemorates the defining moment in all of Jewish history: the giving of the Torah, on Mount Sinai. It's a holiday that tells of God's continuous revelation to the Jewish people. How ironic that it often gets overlooked each year.

Let's take a closer look at Shavuot and try to restore some of the respect it rightfully deserves.

The Back Story

Like the other festivals, Shavuot's observance is mandated in the Torah. The word *Shavuot* means "weeks," because it comes exactly seven weeks after the previous festival of Passover. I'll explain much more about this seven-week period and its significance in chapter 10.

Along with Passover and Sukkot (the flashy siblings), Shavuot is one of the Three Pilgrimage Festivals. As with the other holidays like this, there is an agricultural connection here as well. Sukkot centers around the fall harvest and emphasizes many of the symbols and themes of that season. Passover is known as the Festival of Spring, a time when barley or wheat would be brought as an offering. Similarly, Shavuot celebrates the summer harvest, a time for the first fruits of the season.

Shavuot also commemorates when God gave Moses and the Israelites the Torah, even though that connection is not explicitly given in the text. Rather, the written description of Shavuot seems to be more concerned with the cycle of the farming year and the harvesting of grain and barley.

The Reasons for the Seasons

If Shavuot is truly on par with the other pilgrimage festivals, Passover and Sukkot, then why doesn't it traditionally get the same amount of attention? There are actually a number of reasons.

The Number of Days

Passover and Sukkot are both eight-day festivals. They follow the same pattern of holier days beginning and ending the festival, like bookends, with less sacred intermediate days called *Chol HaMoed* falling in the middle.

In contrast, Shavuot lasts only two days. In fact, like many of the other holidays discussed in this book, only the observance outside of Israel was extended to a second day. The Torah instructs us to celebrate Shavuot for one day. That hardly seems enough time to get into any Shavuot mood. Just when you're in the right frame of mind to observe and celebrate, Shavuot is over.

The Rituals

Let's face it: Shavuot seems boring in comparison with those other festivals. Sukkot is filled with exciting and unusual rituals. We build and dwell in a specially constructed *sukkah* for the duration of the holiday. We incorporate the striking and dramatic lulav and etrog in both individual and public settings. We march around the sanctuary holding those items while praying to God for salvation. As for Passover, it involves a huge amount of preparation. We attend two seders and eat matzah and bitter herbs. We talk about how God performed the defining act of redemption by freeing the Israelites from slavery. I could have easily filled an entire book just talking about those two holidays.

Then there's Shavuot. There are no major symbols or rituals involved. We don't build anything or use any special objects in the service. Sure, the story is exciting (as we'll see), but even so, Passover steals a lot of its thunder. It's tough to compete with the parting of the Red Sea.

The Timing

Sukkot takes place in the fall, right on the heels of Rosh Hashanah and Yom Kippur. Passover is a spring holiday and falls in late March or early April. In fact, many school calendars are set so that the kids' spring break takes place during some part of Passover (and often coinciding with Good Friday and Easter too).

But because Shavuot is a holiday connected with the summer harvest, it falls in late May or early June. By that time, a lot of Hebrew schools have already finished their year or are winding down. Therefore, whereas teachers are likely to spend a lot of time with their students teaching all about Sukkot and Passover, they might give Shavuot only a passing mention, if at all. Kids and adults tend to miss learning much about Shavuot each year, so it often fades into the background.

Sound and Light

Break out the special effects. The giving of the Ten Commandments is surely one of the most dramatic and exciting passages in the entire Torah. The story also contains some fascinating insights into human nature and the very definition of faith.

When last we left the Israelites, they had just successfully crossed the Red Sea and then watched God reverse the miracle and drown the entire Egyptian army. They were duly impressed and grateful, and sang an epic song of thanks to God.

Now what?

Time to get moving again. Shavuot is connected to Passover in that it occurs exactly fifty days (right after the seven-week period) after that holiday. We imagine the same timetable from the Exodus from Egypt to the events surrounding Shavuot.

The Israelites arrive at the foot of Mount Sinai. They are told to make themselves ready and that they need to be washed and pure (meaning no hanky-panky with the wife). Presumably this is intended to keep their heads in the game. Furthermore, they are told not to get too close to the mountain itself, or they'll get divinely zapped. Of course, with the thunder, lightning, and other things that are already taking place, no one wants to get anywhere close to Mount Sinai. The people are terrified of this awe-inspiring demonstration of God's power. And that's saying something after having witnessed the Red Sea split apart.

What follows now is of course one of the most well-known passages of the Bible, transcending many religious traditions. God gives Moses and the people the Ten Commandments. However, the chronology is a little different from what most people have in mind.

On the third day after Moses tells the Israelites to get ready, a trumpet sounds. Back in those times, this might have been a somewhat common occurrence. Before there were air-raid horns or fire alarms, a horn, or shofar (see chapter 1), would be blown to get everyone's attention and to alert them that something major was taking place. This time, though, the sound is different.

Usually when someone blows a trumpet, the sound starts off loud and then eventually tapers off as the person runs out of breath. We read that *this* trumpet sound got louder and stronger the longer it went on. Already the Israelites who are hearing this know something extraordinary is imminent. They realize that this is not an ordinary shofar blast made by a human, but rather a sound coming from God's presence on Mount Sinai.

Moses ascends the mountain, and while there he receives the most famous top-ten list in history. Most depictions of this scene would have us believe that God gave Moses a souvenir of their visit together—two carved tablets to bring down to the Israelites.

Instead, the sequence of events is a little confusing.

It seems that after declaring the Ten Commandments, God goes on—quite a bit. God actually lays out the entire legal basis of Jewish law to Moses. He sets out laws about property, damages, torts, slavery, and, just to keep Moses interested, some prohibitions against forbidden sexual relationships. God also lists the Three Pilgrimage Festivals that are to be observed.

Moses apparently writes all of this down (I assume he brought enough parchment with him), and only after every word is dictated and recorded, God sends him down the mountain to instruct the people. Upon seeing Moses and hearing what God has said, the Israelites announce, "We'll do everything you just said!"

At that point, God summons Moses back up the mountain, reminding everyone else to stay away. Moses takes his sidekick Joshua and proceeds up Mount Sinai. Joshua isn't allowed to go all the way up, so Moses finishes the trip alone.

We're told two things now: first, God gave Moses two carved stone tablets; then, Moses stayed on the mountain forty days and forty nights.

Israelite Idol

A well-known episode now follows, and I think it contains a powerful message about faith that is relevant to every generation.

I N HEBREW, the Ten Commandments are called *Aseret Hadibrot*. That term literally means "ten utterances" or "ten sayings" rather than "ten commandments." Otherwise, they would have been called *Aseret Hamitzvot*.

In fact, the first of the ten isn't a commandment at all. Instead it's a statement:

> I am the Lord your God who brought you out of the land of Egypt and the house of bondage.

That's a powerful opening statement, which gives us the proper context for everything that follows.

It's a curious fact of religious life that this particular list of ten has become so fundamental. They lay a rudimentary foundation of civilization, instructing the Israelites in the basic norms of worship, family, and society.

The Israelites know that Moses has been summoned to the top of Mount Sinai for a forty-day-and-forty-night period. When that time passes, they expect him to return. However, Moses does not return instantly once that period is over. *Immediately*, the Israelites panic. They assume that he is never coming back and that God has abandoned them.

What's interesting here is how fast that reaction takes place. We've all been in a position in which we expect someone to arrive at a certain time. If that person is late, we might get impatient or a little irritated. Eventually, it would even be natural to start worrying.

Granted, the Israelites don't have cell phones and aren't able to call Moses and find out where he is. But very shortly after the precise moment they expect Moses to return from the mountain, the entire people collectively go off the deep end and figure that all is lost and he is never coming back. Incidentally, some commentaries have explained that the people's reaction was a result of miscounting. They got the forty days right but forgot to include the forty nights.

The Israelites converge on Aaron, figuring he would be a natural new leader. They say to Aaron, "Moses isn't coming back. Make us a new god that we can worship."

How do you think Aaron responded? What would *you* say in that situation? Perhaps you'd urge patience. Just give it another day and see if he comes back. No need to panic. Look at what Moses and God have done for us so far.

Instead, without one word of protest, Aaron tells the people to gather up all the gold earrings they can find (from the women *and* the men) and bring them to him. Aaron collects all the gold, puts it in the fire, and out pops the infamous golden calf. All the people announce that this is their new god, and a good old-fashioned pagan celebration follows.

Meanwhile, Moses is preparing to head down the mountain, as originally scheduled. (Remember, the Israelites miscalculated.) God stops him, informs him about what the Israelites have done, and angrily announces that He's had it with this stubborn people. God is ready to wipe them all out and start over with Moses as the head of a new nation.

Moses argues with God. He urges God to have mercy on them, and to remember His promise to Abraham, Isaac, and Jacob. God relents because Moses asks really nicely.

Moses returns down the mountain, witnesses the pagan revelry for himself, and goes ballistic. In extreme anger, he throws the two stone tablets down to the ground and shatters them. Rather strangely, he takes the idol, melts it down, and grinds it into a powder, which he then mixes with water and makes the Israelites consume. Moses separates the camp into two groups—those who are loyal to him and God and those who are not. Then, in a scene left out of a lot of movies and children's books, Moses orders his followers to kill the nonbelievers. We read that about three thousand people died as a result.

Moses asks Aaron, "Why did you do this thing?" Interestingly, Aaron deflects responsibility by responding, "Well, you know how evil all those Israelites are. They told me to do it, so I just went along. Otherwise, I was afraid they were going to kill me." This certainly isn't Aaron's finest moment.

Luckily, Moses purchased the extended protection plan on those tablets. He goes back up the mountain for a free replacement set. Still, God feels the need to rub it in a little by telling Moses that he could have two new tablets to replace the ones "that you broke." Nice.

So what are we to learn from this odd episode? I believe that there is a powerful subtext to this story about the definition of faith.

How often do we hear someone say that he can't believe in God because there's no evidence of His existence? Similarly, a person might declare that if only he could view some proof or miracle, *then* he'd believe in God.

This important story in the Torah so wisely identifies both people's natural yearning for concrete examples and their difficulties in accepting that which they can't see. You might wonder who else but these same Israelites could have a more abiding belief in God, after having personally witnessed the greatest set of miracles ever. If *you* watched the Red Sea part so you could escape from the mightiest army on earth, and then watched the sea close back upon each soldier, don't you think you'd be among the most ardent and zealous believers in God?

Yet not more than a moment after the Israelites thought Moses had abandoned them, they relinquished their belief in an invisible deity and sought a tangible object that they could worship. We learn that faith has nothing to do with so-called evidence. Some will express a belief in God and others cannot. What seems like proof of God's existence to one group of people may be meaningless to another. It's interesting that the Torah had this all figured out so many thousands of years ago.

To Tell the Ruth

Like many other holidays, Shavuot has a parallel story elsewhere in the Bible that serves to highlight a certain theme of the day. On Rosh Hashanah, we read about Abraham nearly sacrificing his son Isaac and we learn the origin of the shofar. Yom Kippur includes the book of Jonah with its themes of repentance. During Sukkot we read the book of Ecclesiastes (or at least try to pronounce it). On Passover we chant the Song of Songs, and on Shavuot it's traditional to read the book of Ruth during services.

The book of Ruth is what I would call a "slice-of-life" story. Unlike other biblical stories that we read, it doesn't contain much action, and there's no violence (although there is some sex to keep everyone interested). It's a calm narrative, set in a pastoral, bucolic environment. If they ever decided to make a movie about certain other parts of the Bible, I could picture that movie showing on HBO, with warnings about graphic violence and it being intended for mature audiences. Ruth, however, would end up on Lifetime.

We are introduced to a typical family: Naomi is married to Elimelech, and they have two sons, Machlon and Kilion. Those two sons are married to Moabite (read: non-Jewish) women, Orpah (no, not *her*—check the spelling) and Ruth, although, interestingly, we don't know which woman is married to which son. I guess it doesn't matter that much, since we immediately learn that all the guys die—first Elimelech, and then the two sons a number of years later.

Naomi is now left with her two Moabite daughters-in-law. She tells them to go and find new husbands who will care and provide for them. But they are fond of Naomi and don't want to go anywhere. Naomi is persistent in explaining that there's no future for these widows with her, an older widow herself with little to no romantic prospects on the horizon. Finally, Orpah reluctantly leaves to make a new life for herself. Ruth, however, will not be swayed, and she announces in a famous passage, "Where you go, I will go. Where you stay, I will stay. Your people are my people and your God will be my God." Now there's a woman who is fond of her mother-in-law.

Naomi and Ruth travel together to Bethlehem, where Elimelech's family came from. Because it's the time of the summer harvest, people are out working in the fields. It was customary back then for the poor to be allowed to follow behind the harvesters and pick up any scraps that had fallen, and this is what Ruth starts doing. As it turns out, this isn't just a random field; it's owned by a relative of Elimelech, a guy named Boaz.

Boaz sees Ruth making her way through his field, harvesting whatever is left behind, and he's drawn to her. He tells her to feel free to continue collecting whatever she can find, and he mentions that

IN DEPTH

T O GET a full understanding of the events in this story and their significance, you have to know about something called *levirate marriage.*

In modern times, couples get married because they've fallen in love (or had one crazy night in Vegas). Not too far back in time, marriages were arranged for economic and political reasons. They were about dynasties, amassing power and wealth, and safeguarding property. In biblical times, men accumulated wealth and property and passed it down to their male heirs. If they didn't have sons, then their possessions would go to other male relatives.

Levirate marriage was instituted to preserve this arrangement. If a guy died, there had to be a way to preserve his property so his wife and *her* family couldn't get their hands on it. Therefore, the widow was obligated to marry the dead husband's brother or another close male relative, so that the line of succession and family inheritance was kept intact. And you thought *your* family was strange.

This is why Naomi initially tried to send Orpah and Ruth away. There was no one around for them to marry, so they would have remained lonely widows their whole lives. Better to go to a new place and start over. Now, upon learning that there's actually a distant relative of her husband's, Naomi is excited because she sees a future for her beloved daughter-in-law.

he has instructed everyone working in the field to leave her alone and not bother her. When Ruth returns home and tells Naomi about this wonderful man she's met, Naomi excitedly explains that Boaz is *mishpacha*, a distant relative!

Naomi now leaves nothing to chance. She instructs Ruth to put on perfume and get herself all gussied up. She is to wait until Boaz has finished his dinner and is relaxing in bed, and then sort of sneak in next to him. The text is not completely clear, but we read that Boaz wakes up in the middle of the night and—surprise!—there's a woman in his bed. Boaz is an old-school gentleman and doesn't make any expected moves (remember, this is Lifetime, not HBO). He has heard about this woman and her loyalty to her mother-in-law, and he is also aware that they are distantly related. Presumably he can do the math on what that means.

The next day, Boaz gathers the town elders and arranges to acquire all property that ever belonged to Elimelech, which, of course, would include the women-folk. In this way, he does the honorable thing and makes an honest woman out of Ruth. They marry and Ruth soon becomes pregnant.

The book concludes with the name of her son and the resulting genealogy. In just a few steps, we get from Ruth's son, Obed, to King David.

So what are we to learn from this very pleasant but not terribly exciting story? Why is it read on Shavuot?

The first connection is the timing of the story. It takes place during the summer harvest season, one of the important themes of Shavuot. That alone might be what initially drew the rabbis to this book and suggested they connect it to Shavuot.

Next, the primary theme of Shavuot is God's giving the Torah to the Israelites and their acceptance of it (except for that Golden Calf thing, but we're willing to overlook that). Ruth does much the same thing when she announces to Naomi that she is willingly accepting Naomi's God and religion. In fact, Ruth is looked upon as the model of the modern convert to Judaism. Prior to this, there was no such thing as conversion. You belonged to whatever tribe or ethnic group in which you were born. In this story, Ruth sets the noble example of a person who is also ready to accept God's Torah, just as the Israelites did.

Finally, the genealogy at the end of the book is important. If not for Ruth's honorable actions, we never would have gotten King David. Furthermore, Jewish tradition tells us that the Messiah will be a descendant of David, so, by extension, it is Ruth, along with her loyalty to Naomi and willingness to embrace the Jewish tradition, who gives us the eventual coming of the Messiah.

The book of Ruth is a seemingly mild story with a powerful moral.

Pull an All-Nighter

Because one of the most vital themes of Shavuot is to demonstrate our enthusiasm to accept God's Torah all over again, it's traditional to have an extended Torah study session on the evening of Shavuot.

Just as the Israelites were ordered to make themselves ready at Mount Sinai during the days ahead of the big event, we try to duplicate that mind-set as well. If we imagine that we ourselves are receiving the Torah on the day of Shavuot, as Moses and the Israelites did, then we anticipate that by doing some study the night before.

This is called *Tikkun Leil Shavuot*, which is a rather interesting choice of words. It means "repair [or fixing] on the evening of Shavuot." Why isn't it simply called something more obvious, like "Torah study"?

I like the idea that the year has come full circle since the last time we commemorated the giving and receiving of the Torah. In that time, we may have forgotten or ignored substantial amounts of the tradition, and we're looking for a way to repair that rift. The word *tikkun* not only means "repair" but also implies something being enhanced or changed for the better. That's what we're aiming for on Shavuot.

Participating in a *Tikkun* doesn't mean you need to stay up all night and walk around like a zombie the next day. While some more-traditional synagogues might indeed hold an all-night event, it's also very common for temples to schedule a study session at a reasonable hour of the evening and lasting for a relatively short time.

During the *Tikkun*, it's traditional to study at least something from every book of the Bible. This might entail learning about a certain theme and tracing it through each book. Some *Tikkun* sessions focus on Jewish music, learning and singing one song whose words come from each successive book of the Bible. The main goal is to look for some new insight into Torah, showing that we're ready to receive it anew each year, and not just to commemorate an ancient historical event.

Dear Dairy

What, you thought I forgot about the food?

Granted, no one was trying to kill us on Shavuot, so the food we eat is not a result of any victory we accomplished over an adversary.

WHY IS there a difference in the requirements of waiting between types of food in order to keep kosher?

If Jewish law says that we are not to mix dairy and meat, then it does make sense that we must wait some length of time after eating meat before we eat something with milk. But wouldn't it similarly make sense to do the opposite?

The laws of *kashrut* purposely make it a little more difficult to eat meat. While the rules of keeping kosher absolutely allow us to eat as much meat as we want (assuming it's kosher meat), we are still supposed to keep in mind that the meat used to be a living animal, and we shouldn't be taking the slaughter of animals for food lightly. This is about Judaism and the laws of keeping kosher putting a slightly higher premium on the consumption of meat and the value of life.

On Shavuot, it is traditional to eat dairy foods. Often this includes cheese blintzes (and no self-respecting Jew will eat those without sour cream) and cheesecake. I believe that all the major diet programs have exemptions for foods eaten for religious purposes. Or at least that's the story I'm sticking with.

Why dairy foods? There's not one definitive answer.

The most common explanation revolves around *kashrut*, the rules and procedures for keeping kosher. According to those rules, when you eat meat, you are required to wait a lengthy period of time (often defined as six hours) before being allowed to eat dairy. This, by the way, is why the refreshments served at temples after services are often parve (not containing meat or milk)—if anyone ate meat before they came to services (like at their Friday night dinner), then eating dairy would force them to be unkosher.

Of course, before the Torah was given, there were no such rules for keeping kosher. So while it's doubtful that the Israelites were relaxing around Mount Sinai enjoying shrimp cocktail, there were certainly no rules yet on the eating of milk and meat together.

All that changed when the Torah was given. Now it became more difficult and even cumbersome to eat meat because you had to do a lot more arranging and figuring in order to plan your next meal. But while the rules say that you have to wait a long time after eating meat before eating dairy, the reverse is not true. It's much simpler to eat dairy foods and not face any restrictions on what you eat later on.

We symbolize this by eating dairy foods during Shavuot, since we're participating in something of a reenactment of receiving the Torah along with its rules on keeping kosher.

Show Me the Green

Another really nice custom on Shavuot is to decorate the temple or sanctuary with plants and flowers. This emphasizes Shavuot's theme of summer harvest and first fruits.

It's not supposed to be anything over the top. A temple might decorate part of the bimah with some flowers or plants. Sometimes the plants can be purchased and taken home by members of the congregation. This is also something that a family can do at home.

This tradition is not without just a little bit of historical controversy, however. At least one Jewish scholar prohibited his community from decorating with plants and flowers because it too closely resembled pagan and non-Jewish customs of the time.

The Bottom Line

It's too bad that Shavuot doesn't get a little more respect.

If the Torah were just a static document, all Hebrew school kids would be forced at one point to make their way through the whole thing—once. We would say, "This is an important Jewish text, it's part of our history, and you should know that it exists. Now let's move on to other subjects."

Instead, we read the Torah over and over. The words don't change from year to year, so what is the point of repeatedly reading the same thing?

The holiday of Shavuot reminds us that it's not the Torah that changes each time we read it; rather, we are the ones who change. The laws, stories, and characters contained inside can be interpreted differently, depending on how you observe or think of Judaism or what kind of community you're in.

In effect, each year on Shavuot we not only read about the Israelites receiving the Torah but we actually receive it for ourselves. We are able to make new connections with the words and decide what we think is important for our lives. It takes the focus off a simply historical event and transforms it into a very personal process.

All that, and you get to eat cheesecake.

CHAPTER 9

TISHA B'AV

THE SADDEST DAY OF THE YEAR

I T SEEMS like every past calamity that affected the Jewish people took place on Tisha B'av. Literally "the ninth of Av," Tisha B'av commemorates a number of different tragedies, both ancient and more modern. Most significantly, Tisha B'av is considered a major fast day, similar to only Yom Kippur in the severity and harshness of its restrictions.

Does that mean there are "minor" fast days? Absolutely. We'll look at them later on in the next chapter and see how they compare to Tisha B'av.

The Back Story

Tisha B'av is fundamentally a day that mourns the destruction of both the First and Second Temples in Jerusalem. The First Temple was destroyed by the Babylonians on the ninth of Av, after which the Jews were forced into exile. Hundreds of years later, the Romans destroyed the Second Temple on the same day, resulting in the scattering of the Jews from the Land of Israel. Both were utterly catastrophic events in Jewish history, involving widespread death and suffering.

Later in history, other terrible things took place on this same day. Each of the following occurred or began in various years, all on the ninth day of Av in the Jewish calendar:

- The beginning of the First Crusade, ultimately resulting in the death of over a million Jews throughout Europe and the Middle East
- The expulsion of Jews from England
- The expulsion of Jews from France
- The expulsion of Jews from Spain
- The official beginning of World War I with Germany's declaration of war against Russia. In addition to a time of suffering for the Jews, this also set the stage for the German role in World War II.

Observances

At its most basic level, Tisha B'av is a fast day. As on Yom Kippur, that observance entails no eating or drinking for about twenty-five hours, from sunset on the first evening to nightfall the next day. As always, this should never endanger anyone's health, so you're allowed to eat if it's medically necessary. Interestingly, the Orthodox rabbinate in Israel also ruled that soldiers in that country are permitted to eat so that they can maintain their strength and readiness.

Additionally, there are other prohibitions that reflect how we view this day and serve to create the appropriate mood.

We are not supposed to wear leather shoes because they are considered a sign of vanity and comfort. All bathing and washing, other than what's necessary for proper hygiene, is against the rules. As expected, sexual relations are out as well.

Surprisingly, you're not supposed to study Torah. This is the only day of the entire year when we're specifically told *not* to engage in the study of Torah or other Jewish texts. Because of the way that the Jewish tradition venerates all aspects of study and Torah, this is truly a remarkable prohibition. Because Torah study is considered such a joyful and pleasurable experience, its inclusion in the list of forbidden activities on Tisha B'av sends a powerful message about how seriously we should look at this day.

There are a few exceptions to the Torah rule. In keeping with the emotion of the day, it is permissible to study particularly sad and depressing books of the Bible, such as Job, Lamentations (which we read in services during the day), and Jeremiah, who might never have smiled once during his entire life.

Services

On Tisha B'av, services look and feel different from those of any other time of the year. The most glaring difference is that for the morning service, one does not put on a tallit (prayer shawl) or the leather straps of tefillin, two rituals that are normally done on any other weekday morning. While putting on tefillin might not be universal—many Jews don't routinely observe this ritual or attend services during the week when they would see it—the wearing of a tallit is something that is much more common and recognized. Especially in a Conservative synagogue, it would be unthinkable to walk into a service and see all the worshippers taking part in the service with no one wearing a tallit. This is exactly what happens on Tisha B'av. It instantly transforms the mood of the prayers into something slightly uncomfortable and unfamiliar.

Some temples might insert special mournful poems and texts into the day's prayers. Most common is the addition of *Eichah*, the book of Lamentations.

This book very vividly describes the events and aftermath of the destruction of the First Temple, with all of its horror and suffering. The main theme of *Eichah* is that of the Temple's destruction and the idea that the resulting exile of the Jews to Babylonia was a result of the people's great sins against God.

During the recitation of this book, and at other times during the day, we engage in traditional rituals associated with mourning. It's customary to sit on low, hard surfaces, as if you were sitting *shiva* (the period of mourning) after the death of a relative. Some people sit right on the floor. Like other books of the Bible, *Eichah* is chanted using a system of cantillation, or trope symbols. While there is one set of melodies used to chant the Torah and another used for a *haftarah* (an excerpt from the Prophets), there is a distinct melody used exclusively for the tropes of *Eichah*, adding to the mood of sadness and mourning.

Additionally, the period leading up to Tisha B'av is marked by notes of sorrow. The three weeks preceding Tisha B'av are treated as a time of mourning. Traditionally, there are no Jewish weddings scheduled for these dates. Each Shabbat, a special *haftarah* is read containing themes of warning and impending doom. Even for those worshippers who don't realize Tisha B'av is on the horizon, the words start painting the picture.

Modern Connections

The fact is that many modern Jews feel no connection to Tisha B'av. It's one thing to intellectually understand that the Jewish people once worshipped at a central shrine—the Temple in Jerusalem. Because it was destroyed (and later rebuilt and destroyed again), the Jewish people's very existence was altered in a profound way. Millions died and suffered. The path of Jewish history changed forever, as the exiled people were forced to leave their homeland.

Today, though, it can be very difficult to tap in to the sadness of Tisha B'av. While some of our prayers do express a yearning to return to the Temple and witness its rebuilding, realistically that's not something most modern Jews are concerned with. All of the observances involving the Temple, including most significantly all of the animal sacrifices, are considered ancient and sometimes irrelevant.

Because of this, a lot of Jews don't see any reason to observe Tisha B'av. While the Temples themselves don't exist anymore, the

Jewish people are thriving, we enjoy religious freedom, and, most notably, we've been back in our Jewish homeland since the establishment of the modern State of Israel. Perhaps Tisha B'av isn't needed anymore.

This isn't a new argument. Even around the time of the Talmud, there were some rabbis who wanted to stop mourning the destruction of the Temples. It wasn't until much later, coinciding with great periods of Jewish suffering in the fifteenth century and later, that Tisha B'av took on a new life and urgency.

One event in Jewish history that so far has been conspicuously absent from this chapter is the Holocaust. How can there be a discussion of the greatest calamities and sufferings to befall the Jewish people without talking about the slaughter of six million Jews during the darkest period of the modern era?

Why isn't the Holocaust remembered during Tisha B'av? If most modern Jews feel little to no connection with Tisha B'av, then wouldn't linking it with the Holocaust be the logical choice?

As I'll point out in chapter 10, that's precisely what some people suggested doing in the wake of World War II. During the 1950s, the Israeli Knesset decided to create an official day on which to remember the Holocaust (later called Yom HaShoah). One option was to incorporate its remembrance into the already profoundly sad day of Tisha B'av. However, precisely because many Jews already viewed Tisha B'av as a Temple-centered holiday, the Knesset felt that a more modern day was warranted, one that even secular Jews could connect with, unattached in any way to what they thought was an ancient and anachronistic observance of the Temple period.

The Bottom Line

It seems, then, that Tisha B'av is a day on the calendar that is of importance only to those Jews who find a connection to the Temple. Other Jews are able to find meaning in more modern occasions like Yom HaShoah, or even Yom Hazikaron (Israeli Memorial Day, also discussed in chapter 10). How many days of mourning do we need in the Jewish calendar?

I believe that one reason why Tisha B'av has endured long after Temple times is that a lot of Jews are less concerned with the actual, literal remembrance of the destruction of the Temples, and are more moved by the need to have one all-encompassing day of mourning for sad events throughout Jewish history. Perhaps it's not the events themselves that are the focus. Instead, Jews can relate to the raw emotion of the day. Taking Tisha B'av together with the other festivals and holidays of the calendar, a Jew can experience the natural progression of the year, ranging from solemnity, joy, awe, and gratitude to utmost sadness.

Finally, there are definitely some modern, relevant messages that we can take from Tisha B'av. According to tradition, there were two distinct reasons why God punished the Jewish people with the destruction of each Temple. The first time, we learn that it was the people's sinning and turning their backs on God's laws that brought about His anger. While this may seem a little too vengeful for modern sensibility, it does teach us that actions have consequences.

The fall of the Second Temple also imparts a powerful message. Its destruction was thought to be a result of infighting and endless squabbling among the Jews of that time. We learn about *sin'at chinam*, baseless hatred of others. In other words, this Temple fell because it couldn't be sustained from the inside. From this story we can be introduced to the theme of *shalom bayit*, or peace and tranquility at home, both within our families and with others whom we know.

CHAPTER 10

CALENDAR ODDITIES, MINUTIAE, AND MISCELLANY

JUDAISM'S OWN ADVENT CALENDAR AND OTHER ASSORTED FUN FACTS

I T'S EASY to focus on the big holidays, like Rosh Hashanah, Yom Kippur, and Passover, and feel like you have a decent understanding of the Jewish year. But to truly feel connected to the cycle of Jewish holidays, it really helps to have a basic understanding of the Jewish calendar and how Jewish rituals and observances adjust to the different time periods.

Let's first take a very basic look at how the Jewish calendar works. I promise that you won't need a calculator or an advanced degree in astronomy to learn the fundamentals.

Bella Luna

If you really want the simplest way to figure out the Jewish calendar, then step outside on a clear evening and look up. The moon will tell you everything you need to know.

There, that's it. I told you it was going to be a basic look at the calendar.

The Jewish calendar is lunar, meaning its months are based on the cycle of the moon. When a Jewish month starts, there's a new moon. In the middle of a Jewish month, there's a full moon. Furthermore, many Jewish holidays occur in the middle of the month, when there's a full moon, making it pretty easy to figure out when the holidays fall.

For example, I can be on vacation in August, enjoying the late summer weather and walking around in the evening, and as I look up I observe that the moon is just a sliver. I realize, "Hey, that means exactly one month until Rosh Hashanah!" (This tends to drive my family crazy.)

Since I know (and now so do you after reading chapter 1) that Rosh Hashanah is the Jewish New Year and falls on the first of the month, then there must be a new moon when it starts. Each Jewish month goes from one new moon to the next. So while most normal people would enjoy the night air and the feeling of being away, I'm thinking that I have about twenty-nine or so days to make sure I'm ready for Rosh Hashanah.

I didn't need to consult a Jewish calendar or do a lot of counting in my head. One look up at the moon told me everything I needed to know.

In ancient times, this was a logical way to mark the passage of time. Everyone, regardless of whether they were literate, educated, or had access to information or technology, could look up at night and see what the moon looked like. It's not an accident that a lot of Jewish holidays tend to fall on the fourteenth or fifteenth of the Jewish month. It makes it a lot easier to know that a certain observance is supposed to begin when there's a full moon.

Additionally, when there was significant travel required, like for the Three Pilgrimage Festivals, it was especially helpful to have the bright light of a full moon to help with moving around at night.

Count On It

Have you ever been so excited about something in the future that you literally counted the days until it was time? Kind of like an Advent calendar? Such a thing exists in the Jewish calendar.

The *Omer* is a forty-nine-day period that falls between the festivals of Passover and Shavuot. Like many other aspects of the Jewish calendar, this is based on an ancient agricultural schedule, but it contains a powerful religious and spiritual message as well. The Omer period itself has a distinct mood, and there are some notable commemorations that fall within these forty-nine days.

The Back Story

The Torah tells us that we are supposed to count fifty days, beginning with the day after Passover. We are to keep track of seven weeks (there's forty-nine days), and on the next day (fifty), we celebrate a festival, and we refrain from work because it's a holy day.

On the second day of Passover, which would be the first day of the Omer period, the Jews were instructed to bring a portion (literally, an *omer*) of barley to the Temple in Jerusalem. At the conclusion of the seven weeks, on the holiday of Shavuot, a wheat offering was to be brought.

If all this sounds just a little too farm-like to you, remember that the cycle of the Jewish calendar revolves around agricultural life. The Three Pilgrimage Festivals—Sukkot, Passover, and Shavuot—each represent an important harvesttime for Jews living in the ancient Land of Israel.

Think how much sense this makes.

Today, people observe the passing of the year in different ways. Some people keep it simple and mentally go from January through December. Corporate workers might keep their minds on the fiscal year. Accountants tend to think from one April to the next. Countless kids and families live by the school calendar, which itself hearkens back to the same agricultural year reflected in the Jewish calendar.

Just as kids trace their progress through the school year with vacations and grading periods, along with the change in weather from cool to cold to warm (making them look forward to the summer), the ancient Jews did the same thing with the fall harvest (Sukkot), the renewal of spring (Passover), and the bringing of the first fruits (Shavuot). Between the growth of their crops and the phases of the moon that they would constantly observe, they very accurately marked the passage of the months and years.

There's a spiritual parallel to this as well.

Since most of us are not particularly consumed with the agricultural calendar—it's easy enough to harvest anything we want at the supermarket—we find a way to connect the Omer to something religious. Specifically, we concentrate on the Israelites' journey from Egypt to Mount Sinai where they received the Torah. Passover, the festival that celebrates the liberation from slavery, marks the beginning of the Omer. Then, seven weeks later, we celebrate Shavuot, which recalls the giving of the Torah at Sinai. Counting the period of time between the two holidays was the rabbis' way of linking them thematically and providing a spiritual connection between them.

A Number of Things

Perhaps the easiest way to observe the Omer period is to count. After all, that's the literal and exact instruction that we read in the Torah. Count each day of the seven weeks.

How do we do that? Should we wake up in the morning, stumble out of bed, and say, "Day 38. Where's my coffee?"

That's actually pretty close. (Coffee is optional.)

First, remember that all Jewish days begin at sundown. So if you look at a Jewish calendar to see what the date is today, you should realize that it's only that date until this evening, when the sun goes down.

Then it's already tomorrow. Today started last night, after yesterday. This utterly confused a Hebrew school class I once taught.

Since we're supposed to show some enthusiasm for observing the Torah's commandments, we should perform this one and count each day of the Omer *as soon as that day starts*. That means just after sunset. Because this is a specific commandment from the Torah, there is a blessing recited over the counting, which can be found in any prayer book.

Additionally, there's a set way to count, which is also written down very clearly in the prayer book. You're supposed to say what day of the Omer it is, and then break that down into weeks and days. If I didn't know better, I'd have bet that the entire ritual of counting the Omer was something started by *Sesame Street*.

So instead of saying, "Hey, it's Day 38," we recite, "Today is thirty-eight days, which is five weeks and three days of the Omer."

In chapter 8, I bemoaned the fact that Shavuot suffers from a general lack of respect. It doesn't get the attention it deserves being a major festival and commemorating such a transformative event as the giving of the Torah to the Israelites. Counting the Omer is one way to remedy that. We not only celebrate Shavuot when it occurs, but we also anticipate its coming by literally counting the days until it's here.

Religious observance works best when a person can directly relate to the themes and rituals of the holiday rather than viewing them as a bunch of random acts that someone came up with thousands of years ago. One of the specific goals of Passover is to sit at the seder table and not just recall the period of slavery, but actually imagine that *we ourselves* were slaves. The Omer lets us take this one step further, by forcing us to think about what it would be like to be suddenly liberated, wandering through a strange wilderness, and seeking guidance. Previously, the only directions for living that the slaves received were through their Egyptian taskmasters. But can lifelong slaves really make the switch to independent thinking so fast?

So for the next seven weeks, they made their way from the bonds of slavery to the foot of Mount Sinai, where they were to receive the commandments. By counting each of those forty-nine days, we mentally trace that progress from slavery to freedom.

Like some other seemingly random commandments found in the Torah, there's a lot of insight and wisdom built into the counting of the Omer, and you don't need to be a farmer to fully appreciate it.

Mourning Has Broken

Getting married sometime soon? Better check the calendar.

In addition to its agricultural roots and the religious anticipation of Shavuot, the Omer is also traditionally observed as a period of semi-mourning. According to a story in the Talmud, 24,000 students of Rabbi Akiva, an important figure and teacher of the time, died of a plague that took place during the Omer. In recognition of that tragedy, it's traditional for some people to practice certain customs related to mourning during the seven weeks.

One of the more common customs that you may come across is that there are traditionally no Jewish weddings performed during the Omer. Often a couple will come in to see their rabbi or cantor and discuss the planning of their wedding. The first thing that everyone will check is the suggested date and time of year for the ceremony. If it falls between Passover and Shavuot, it usually means that you have to look for another date. (Or another rabbi. This is common in more traditional branches of Judaism but may not be observed at all within the liberal branches.)

I always found it interesting that one could see this firsthand when browsing through the wedding announcements of a major urban newspaper like the *New York Times*. It's fairly easy to figure out which of those announcements involve Jewish couples. Right around the time of the Omer, during what would normally be the most popular time of the year for weddings to take place, all of a sudden there are significantly fewer Jewish names. This shows that while the average person probably doesn't worry too much about the minutiae of Omer observance, the tradition revolving around scheduling Jewish weddings outside of this period endures.

Similarly, some observant Jews will avoid any celebrations at all during the Omer. Usually, they'll define "celebration" as any event that includes music. So someone might attend a bar mitzvah, for instance, but then not show up at a reception where music will be played. Likewise, those who observe the Omer in this way would also not be present at any sort of concert.

Are you depressed enough yet? There's more. Traditionally, one would also refrain from getting a haircut or wearing new clothes during this time. Both of those things are symbols of vanity and wanting to look nice, something not usually done during periods of mourning.

I know what you're thinking: Seven weeks without a haircut? Not to worry—there are a couple of loopholes built in. We'll get to them a little later. I promise that no one needs to look like the Wolf Man by the end of the Omer.

The Three Yoms of the Omer

There are three important days in the Jewish calendar that take place during the Omer. I've nicknamed them the "Three Yoms [Days] of the Omer" because their names all start the same way. They are

Yom HaShoah (Holocaust Remembrance Day)
Yom Hazikaron (Memorial Day)
Yom Ha'atzma'ut (Independence Day)

Let's look at each one and its importance within the Jewish calendar.

Yom HaShoah

At first glance, it seems strange that there would be one day set aside to remember the millions of victims who perished during the *Shoah*, the Holocaust. After all, the genocide of World War II took place over the course of many years. How do you choose one specific day on which to formally remember those who died? Furthermore, since we already have a day in the Jewish calendar dedicated to the remembrance of tragedies throughout thousands of years of Jewish history, Tisha B'av (see chapter 9), wouldn't it make perfect sense to add this latest horror to our collective recollection?

The date of Yom HaShoah falls about two weeks after the start of Passover, and its selection was indeed significant. During the Shoah, there was one famous example of Jewish resistance to the Nazis, known as the Warsaw Ghetto Uprising. The Warsaw Ghetto was one of many such areas where Jews were forced to live in crowded and deplorable conditions. Eventually, the Nazis would liquidate these ghettos by rounding up all of the residents and transporting them to concentration camps.

When word came that the Nazis were planning to do this to the Jews of the Warsaw Ghetto, the people living there decided to fight back rather than submit to deportation from the ghetto and an almost certain death in concentration camps. Ultimately, of course, a relatively small group of poorly armed and malnourished fighters was no match for the might of the German army. But against all odds they were able to fight for weeks, inflicting casualties and damage upon the Germans by using crudely assembled explosive devices and whatever weapons they were able to smuggle in from outside the walls.

Yom HaShoah falls on the anniversary of this heroic event. In fact, the holiday's full name (which people don't commonly use) is Yom HaShoah U'Gevurah (Day of the Holocaust and Heroism). I think it was a brilliant choice to link an event of such utmost horror and darkness to a strong example of Jewish strength and resistance. It inserts what might be the one positive spark of hope and pride that could exist during a time of such dread.

That doesn't mean that the date is without controversy.

We're used to religious observances being based on ancient events and texts. When the Torah mandates that a certain day and month should be observed as a holiday, we pretty much know what to do. Then later, the rabbis of the Talmud would decide upon details of its observance and how to perform the rituals. There would be texts and prayers that we add to our services. While there might be some difference of opinion on specific points, the major details were decided and fixed a long time ago.

But how do you create a Jewish holiday or event from scratch in modern times?

In the early 1950s, the Israeli Knesset decided to institute this day of Holocaust remembrance and determined that it would be set in the Jewish calendar on its current day of the twenty-seventh of Nisan. The Orthodox Jews of Israel felt that this was an inappropriate date because one should rejoice during Nisan, the month of Passover. Furthermore, they felt that Tisha B'av was the more logical choice, since it already involved fasting and mourning. They also didn't recognize that a secular body (the Israeli Parliament) had the authority to establish a date of Jewish religious significance.

The counterargument is that Tisha B'av is a fast day centered around Jerusalem and the destruction of the First and Second Temples. Those events, while historically tragic, simply don't resonate as strongly among modern Jews. In contrast, the Shoah is recent and raw. There are countless Jewish families that have been directly affected by this horror. It became clear that a separate and distinct day, unconnected with ancient Jerusalem, was needed.

Because the commemoration is so young, there also hasn't been an opportunity for one set list of accepted rituals to develop. We may know that it's Yom HaShoah, but what do we do?

Some common practices have evolved over the years. First, it's traditional and meaningful to light a special type of *yahrzeit candle* for the twenty-four-hour period of Yom HaShoah. A yahrzeit candle is usually a small, white candle contained in a jar, and one would light it on the anniversary of a family member's death, according to the Jewish calendar. On Yom HaShoah, temples will often distribute these candles, but with yellow-colored wax. This is a remembrance of

I N ISRAEL, the observance of Yom HaShoah is striking and unforgettable.

The population in Israel can often be divided into two disparate factions: religious and secular. During any holiday or festival, secular Jews do not necessarily mark any observance at all other than enjoying a day off from work or school. To them, knowing that they're Jewish and living in Israel is a sufficient display of their Judaism. They leave any religious practice to the Orthodox sect.

So it's pretty remarkable for a day on the Jewish calendar to bridge that gap and connect virtually all Israelis, and, indeed, all Jews around the world. Yom HaShoah is such an event. Regardless of any religious background, this is a day that profoundly affects a great segment of the world's Jewish population. In particular, a huge segment of Israel's citizens are direct descendants of European Jews or first-generation immigrants themselves.

On the morning of Yom HaShoah, a siren sounds in Israel for two minutes. This siren is heard throughout the entire country, sounded by every air-raid horn and played on every radio or television station. During these two minutes, the entire country comes to a stop and observes a moment of silence. Traffic halts and people stand next to their cars. All activities—shopping, playing, learning, eating—stop while everyone stands quietly. Busy highways become temporary parking lots. It's an incredibly powerful and meaningful show of respect and sadness.

the yellow stars that the European Jews were forced to wear, one of the most identifiable symbols of the Shoah. Synagogues or individuals might even light six of these candles, all lined up in a row, as a vivid reminder of the six million Jews who perished.

Some Jews do fast for part of the day, even though there's no specific direction to do so. They might also refrain from entertainment or recreational activities. In some modern prayer books, there are additional texts that might be added to that day's service.

Yom Hazikaron

We have Memorial Day in the United States as well, and it's always observed on the last Monday of May. Just as in Israel, this day is set aside to remember all the soldiers who have died throughout the country's history.

In this country, how do we traditionally observe it?

Most people don't at all. In fact, Memorial Day has been dubbed the unofficial start of summer. Many people enjoy the day off, hope for warm weather, and head to the beach or schedule a barbeque. We know, vaguely, that there are somber ceremonies that take place involving civic officials and gray-haired veterans, but they don't typically figure too prominently in our plans.

In Israel, however, it could not be more different. Yom Hazikaron, Israeli Memorial Day, is another profoundly sad day in the calendar. Just like on Yom HaShoah a week earlier, a siren goes off and marks a two-minute moment of silence throughout the entire country. Yom Hazikaron is observed each year on the day before Yom Ha'atzma'ut, Independence Day.

Why does Memorial Day in Israel seem to matter so much more than in this country?

Israel is a small country, about the size of New Jersey. So imagine that you live in the Country of New Jersey, and for the last sixty-something years, you've been at war with neighboring Delaware, Pennsylvania, and New York. It would be easy to see how in a state so small, you would quickly know of someone who died fighting during that time. More likely, you would have a direct connection to a fallen soldier.

That's the situation in Israel. Yom Hazikaron is not just a civic event. It's deeply personal. People don't mourn the *idea* of soldiers being killed in battle; they mourn their sons and daughters.

Yom Ha'atzma'ut

Israeli Independence Day falls on fifth day of Iyar, the Hebrew anniversary of the signing of Israel's Declaration of Independence in 1948. As you might imagine, it is one of the most joyous and celebrated days of the Jewish calendar in Israel and among Jews throughout the world.

Because Yom Ha'atzma'ut comes right on the heels of Yom Hazikaron, there's quite a shift in the national mood. Israelis mark one of the saddest days of the year, and as soon as sunset takes place, they immediately shift gears and proceed to celebrate.

Isn't that a tough thing to do? Of course, Yom Ha'atzma'ut must be celebrated on the fifth of Iyar because that date was when the Declaration was signed. (It's the same reason why you couldn't celebrate the Fourth of July on any other day than July 4.) But surely Yom Hazikaron could have been put anywhere in the calendar since it's not tied to one specific event. Ostensibly, it seems like an odd choice to schedule two such fundamentally opposite days back to back.

In fact, it's a logical and sensitive decision. In the midst of sadness, people who mourn for those who have given their lives for the State of Israel are looking for some reason why their loved ones did not die in vain. What better way can there be to demonstrate that fact than the celebration of Israel's independence and continued existence? Rather than causing an awkward shift in emotion, I imagine that the joy of Yom Ha'atzma'ut helps to bring enormous comfort to all the citizens who remember a fallen soldier.

As we've seen with other recent additions to the Jewish calendar, there is no fixed list of rituals that are observed on Yom Ha'atzma'ut. Some temples have a custom to add certain prayers, usually a recitation of *Hallel*, a set of psalms that are recited on other holidays.

Get Fired Up

In addition to these three days, there is another significant day that takes place during the Omer: *Lag B'Omer*. This holiday is so named because Hebrew letters also have a corresponding numerical value. The Hebrew letters *lamed* (30) and *gimmel* (3) come together to form *lag* (33). Therefore, *Lag B'Omer* simply means "the thirty-third day of the Omer."

What's so special about this one day out of the whole forty-nine?

Hopefully you remember what I told you about the plague that killed 24,000 of Rabbi Akiva's students. That's the basis for observing some traditional mourning practices during this time. But happily, on the thirty-third day of the Omer, the plague stopped and no one else died. On this day, we suspend all demonstrations of mourning. If you can work out the details, feel free to get married on *Lag B'Omer*. A little less dramatically, you can also get a haircut. (See, I told you that there'd be a loophole.)

There's no religious significance to *Lag B'Omer*. It's become a recreational day when people are encouraged to participate in outdoor activities. Religious schools might hold an outdoor field day for the students. In Israel, there are often outdoor events scheduled, and at night it's common for people to light bonfires.

Matz-a-Going On?

I'm just including this one in here in case you ever wanted to impress someone at a cocktail party with your detailed knowledge of the Jewish calendar.

One more day that falls within the Omer is called *Pesach Sheni*—literally, "the second Passover." As if your digestive system weren't already traumatized enough from eight days of eating matzah-based products, exactly one month after Pesach, on the fourteenth day of Iyar, some people will eat matzah again.

Part of the original instructions for Passover during Temple times was to eat the special Pesach sacrifice. Pilgrims would make their way to Jerusalem in observance of this holiday specifically to fulfill this commandment. Circumstances, however, might have prevented some people from completing the journey. Perhaps they were ill and couldn't make the trip.

Another reason has to do with purity. In those days, Jews had to maintain a state of ritual purity, which could be accomplished through making proper sacrifices at the certain times and not coming into contact with some forbidden things, such as a dead body. If they did become ritually impure, they'd have to go through prescribed steps in order to become pure again.

One consequence of being ritually impure was that a person would be ineligible to eat the Passover sacrifice (maybe because no one wanted to sit near him at the table). The calendar gave these people one more chance to complete their obligation. On Pesach Sheni, they could perform this ritual.

Because there is no longer any Temple in Jerusalem, we don't worry about ritual purity. Luckily, we also don't have to clean our houses and empty out every cupboard again for just one day.

Tree at Last

....

It's time to branch out into another subject. Within the Jewish calendar, we have yet another type of New Year. How many does that make?

There are actually three important occasions in the Jewish calendar that are considered New Years. While this might sound strange, we basically do the same thing today. While January 1 is celebrated as the official New Year's Day, many people, including most kids, also think about the first day of school as being a type of New Year. Any accountants reading this now will think about when their fiscal year begins, and realize they treat that as a kind of New Year. There are different dates for different purposes, and the Jewish calendar is no different.

First, we have the obvious New Year, Rosh Hashanah, discussed at length in chapter 1. As one would expect, the first day of the first month of any calendar would properly be designated as the New Year. Rosh Hashanah, the first day of the month of Tishrei, is the Jewish New Year, and it occurs sometime in September.

Next, remembering what we learned about the festival of Passover in chapter 7, we know that in the Bible, the month of Nisan was regarded as the first month of the year. That would make the first day of Nisan, which typically falls in late March or early April, another candidate for the New Year.

We're not done yet. There is a third New Year, this one set aside just for trees. Yes, you read that right. Trees get their own New Year and birthday. It's called *Tu Bishevat*, which means "the fifteenth of Shevat." This typically occurs in late January or early February.

Isn't anyone asking the obvious question: Why would trees need a birthday?

The Bark Story

It turns out that the Torah contains a strong environmental message.

In Leviticus, the Israelites are told that when they plant all kinds of trees, they are not allowed to eat or otherwise use any of the fruit from those trees for the first three years. Then, during the fourth year, the fruit is considered holy, to be set aside for God and not to be eaten. This, of course, is an acknowledgment that the tree and everything that comes from it is really from God. That's a message that the

Torah tells us many times throughout the year. So when the Temple was standing, people would bring these fourth-year fruits to Jerusalem and dedicate them to God.

Finally, in the fifth year, you could enjoy a nice fruit salad. At that time, it would be permissible to eat any of the fruit from the trees that were planted.

As a practical matter, this series of instructions makes a lot of sense. It takes some time for a tree to produce fruit that's mature and will taste its best. This way, the Israelites had to restrain themselves from picking fruit from trees prematurely and possibly compromising how those trees would grow in future years.

As you read all this, I wonder if you're picturing your backyard. One year, you go back there, dig a hole, and plant some kind of fruit-bearing tree that you picked up at the greenhouse. Now it's a fairly simple task to watch that tree over the course of time, see when it begins to produce fruit, and start your count of years. You know that Jewish law tells you that only during the fifth year are you allowed to pick that fruit and eat it.

Now pretend that you own an orchard.

Your job just got a lot more complicated. I suppose that it would theoretically be possible for you to make your way down each path, row after row of trees, and mark each tree with its year of planting. Since we're living in modern times, perhaps you could number each of the possibly thousands of trees in your orchard and keep track of them all by using a spreadsheet.

In order to fully observe this important commandment, you'd have to know the planting date (i.e., the birthday) of *every tree*. That sounds impossibly difficult and unwieldy. Luckily, Tu Bishevat makes all that unnecessary. It's the one birthday for all the trees. On this day in the Jewish calendar, the fifteenth day of Shevat, every tree automatically becomes one year older. Quick and simple.

To take the extreme examples, if you planted a tree on the day before Tu Bishevat, on the next day that tree would be considered a one-year-old tree. Similarly, a tree planted on the day *after* Tu Bishevat would have to wait a full year before being the same age. It's probably a good thing that we don't use the same system for people.

Even though Tu Bishevat stems from a commandment in Leviticus, there's no mention of this day in the Torah. There are no set laws or obligations associated with it, although some customs have become popular, as we'll see. In fact, it was only during Talmudic times that the rabbis came up with the notion of trees having their own New Year. After some of the usual bickering between a couple schools of thought, the choice of the fifteenth of Shevat won out.

Save the Trees

There's another important passage in the Torah that mentions trees, and its powerful message tells us a lot about how the Jewish religion viewed not only trees themselves but also the environment as a whole.

In Deuteronomy, the Israelites are told that when they go to war against a city, they should take special care to not destroy trees in the process.

At first glance, that seems like a pretty strange instruction. It's acceptable to wage war, which presumably involves capturing and killing many people, but make sure that you don't needlessly harm trees.

The text then goes on to ask the rhetorical question: "Are trees people, that you should lay siege against them?" This suggests that the Torah is looking at the bigger picture. It's acknowledging that people come and go—they wage war and conquer cities—on a different scale of time from the trees and the earth.

In the next verse, the Torah backtracks a bit and says that it's actually OK to cut down trees that you need for building. Only the trees that produce fruit for eating should be protected. This nicely combines the practical and sensible use of trees with the Torah's environmental message.

Tu Bishevat Today

You may be thinking that all of this sounds interesting, but so what? We don't live with a Temple in Jerusalem anymore, most of us don't own orchards, and we can get all the fruit we need at the local supermarket.

Actually, there are a number of ways that Tu Bishevat is relevant today.

IN DEPTH

THERE'S A well-known story from the Talmud that further gives us an idea of how Judaism thinks about trees and the environment.

According to this story, there once was an old man planting a carob tree. A young guy saw him working and toiling and wondered why he was expending so much effort.

"Old man," the kid said. "Why are you knocking yourself out like that? Do you think you're going to be around when this tree is grown?" (What a polite and considerate young man.)

"No," the elderly gentleman replied. "But just as others before me planted trees so I could enjoy them, I, too, will plant a tree for others."

This very simple story contains a powerful message about protecting and preserving the environment for future generations. It reminds us that Tu Bishevat is a "big picture" day rather than a time to focus only on the present.

First, it's traditional to plant trees on this day, especially in Israel. This can often be accomplished through the Jewish National Fund (JNF). It's very common for people to pay a small fee to JNF, which uses the funds to plant trees and populate forests in Israel. It's even nicer when you designate "your" tree in honor of a special occasion or in memory of a loved one.

Second, Tu Bishevat is an appropriate day to be aware of the environment. It's Judaism's own Earth Day, a time to look at how we treat our natural surroundings and resources. In this context, we remember that what we have comes from God.

Not a Hot Date

Consider the date chosen for this New Year for trees, the fifteenth of Shevat. Depending upon where in the world you live, that might seem somewhat illogical.

THERE'S A well-known passage in the Torah that, while possibly troubling in its literal meaning, always makes me think of Tu Bishevat.

In the second paragraph of the Shema, taken from Deuteronomy, we read that God expects us to obey His commandments. If we do so, we're told, we will be awarded with rain at the proper time, and with an abundant harvest and plenty to eat. If, however, we violate the commandments, God will hold back the rain. Crops will wither, and we won't have enough to eat. Eventually, we'll perish and disappear from the land that God gave us.

This seems pretty harsh. "Do what I say," God is telling us, "and nobody gets hurt."

There are many ways to interpret this text. Still, especially within the Reform movement, many prayer books omit this passage because it reflects an anachronistic and monolithic view of reward and punishment. Real life contains a lot more nuance than that.

I've always thought there was a pro-environmental message hiding between the lines. There are many ways that humans affect the environment. Without dipping my foot into the controversial and political waters of global warming, I think it's safe to say that there are certainly examples of humankind having an effect on our natural resources. Maybe the text warning that our disobedience to the Torah will result in the rains being held back is in fact an admonition against irresponsible treatment of the earth and the environment.

In addition to making a donation to JNF, a lot of people feel it's important to personally plant a new tree. Many synagogues, often with students of their Hebrew school, will go outside and plant a tree in observance of Tu Bishevat.

In January?

That may not be exactly prime tree-planting weather. In many parts of the world, you can't even get a shovel to penetrate the frozen

PERFECT FOR FAMILIES

KIDS ARE already used to observing a day like Tu Bishevat. Throughout their years in school, they learn about the environment, and they learn to conserve and recycle. Some schools make a big deal out of Earth Day, a relatively recent addition to the calendar in mid-April that teaches a lot of the same themes as Tu Bishevat, but in a secular context. Tu Bishevat is a great opportunity to build on what kids already know about the earth and its climate and resources, and then connect it to Judaism.

One creative method that has become popular is holding a "Tu Bishevat Seder" modeled on the well-known Passover observance. This specific seder is centered around the cycle of the year and the growth of different fruits and other foods, and it has become an increasingly popular addition to Hebrew school programs.

At a Tu Bishevat seder, we drink four cups of wine, just like on Passover. But here, each cup combines a mixture of red and white wine or juice, so that the color changes each time, symbolizing the progression of different seasons throughout the year. We also include certain foods, based on a passage in Deuteronomy that describes the Land of Israel as a "land of wheat and barley, of vines, figs, and pomegranates, a land of olive trees and honey." Kids can be encouraged to try something new or unfamiliar (good luck with that).

It's clear that modern-day observances of Tu Bishevat have evolved a long way past keeping track of how old your tree is.

earth in January, even if you're able to clear the snow away. The rabbis could have chosen *any* date—why not a beautiful day in summer when everyone already wants to be outside?

As we've seen, the Jewish calendar revolves around the agricultural cycle of Israel. So even though many of us here in North America on the fifteenth of Shevat are enduring the dead of winter, in Israel, they're in the middle of the rainy season. It's a perfect time to get trees in the ground before the warmer and dryer weather takes over.

The Minor Fasts

Sure, you can imagine fasting on Yom Kippur, the Day of Atonement. After all, our very survival is at stake based on our own actions and choices.

Then there's Tisha B'av, the saddest day on the Jewish calendar.

Are there really more days throughout the year when we're supposed to fast?

The answer is yes, even though many Jews don't know much about these days, and even fewer actually fast.

There are five of these so-called minor fasts in the Jewish calendar. On each of these days, Jews are supposed to fast, but the severity is nothing like Yom Kippur or Tisha B'av. Instead, the fast only lasts from the break of day until nightfall. So it's perfectly fine to set your alarm and get up before sunrise in order to eat a big breakfast. Also, it's possible to break the fast earlier in the afternoon by studying Torah or another text and then having a meal of some kind.

Let's look at each of the different minor fasts and see why they're included in the calendar. Interestingly, some of them don't stand on their own, but are connected to the main observance of a major holiday. It's important to at least be aware of these minor fasts because they round out the cycle of Jewish observance and give an understanding of what the rabbis thought was significant. These occasions help to expand our observance of certain holidays and develop some of their important themes.

The Fast of Gedaliah

This takes place the day after Rosh Hashanah, although it has nothing to do with that holiday. It recalls the killing of a guy named Gedaliah, who was a Jewish governor in Judah.

The Tenth of Tevet

On this date in the Jewish calendar, we remember the events that eventually led to the destruction of the First Temple. It was on this day that the Babylonians began their siege of Jerusalem.

The Fast of Esther

This occurs on the thirteenth of Adar, the day just before Purim. It recalls that Esther and the rest of the Jews fasted for three days (I don't know how they pulled that off) when they learned of Haman's genocidal plans.

The Fast of the Firstborn

If you're a younger sibling in your family, you've got a pass on this one. On the day before Passover, it's traditional for all firstborn males to fast, in remembrance and gratitude that only the Egyptian firstborn males were killed in the last plague. All the Hebrew firstborn males were spared.

The Seventeenth of Tammuz

Again, this is related to Tisha B'av. On this day, the walls of Jerusalem were breached, leading to the destruction of the Second Temple.

Also, this date occurs exactly forty days after the festival of Shavuot (chapter 8), on which God presented Moses with a legendary set of tablets. Forty days after that, Moses descended the mountain and found the Israelites having the most famous house party in history, complete with golden calf. Upon seeing this, he smashed the tablets on the ground in anger.

This fast commemorates that inauspicious event also.

The Bottom Line

Think of the Jewish calendar as a solid wall made up of many bricks. It's stood in the same place for thousands of years, enduring throughout the generations. You might think of each major festival or holiday as a brick in that wall.

Similarly, these other occasions of calendar miscellany, while not accorded the same importance as the major festivals, are nonetheless vital to our wall's existence—they're the mortar that connects the bricks to each other and gives the Jewish calendar its strength and timelessness.

A lot of Jewish homes have a Jewish calendar hanging up. Rather than necessarily being a symbol of religious observance, the calendar helps connect a person to the rhythm of the Jewish cycle of holidays and events, the ebb and flow of emotion from joyous to reserved, from sacred to routine.

APPENDIX I

YOUR QUICK AND HANDY GUIDE TO ALL THE HOLIDAYS

ARE YOU having trouble remembering every last detail about each holiday? This appendix is for you.

What follows is a quick and simple listing of all the major holidays discussed in this book, complete with their most common symbols or practices, ritual items, and, of course, traditional foods. You can use this section as a handy reference when you want to refresh your memory about a certain festival or holiday. In Appendix II, I'll list each of the Jewish months and the Jewish holidays that take place at those times.

Rosh Hashanah

What

Jewish New Year

Why

Mentioned in the Torah as a holy day, but with no original connection to its being the New Year.

When

September

Symbols and Practices

- Shofar: The ram's horn is blown throughout the holiday, as a symbol of alert and calling the Jewish people to attention.
- *Teshuvah*: Repentance, the act of looking over our deeds of the past year and finding ways to make amends to those we've hurt. We should also seek to improve our lives and ensure that we don't fall back into the same patterns.
- The Book of Life: On Rosh Hashanah, tradition holds that we pray to have our names inscribed in this book so we'll be around next year.
- The Binding of Isaac: A heart-warming family story of blind obedience, attempted filicide, and lasting estrangement that gives us the origin of the shofar, and why we use it on this day.

Let's Eat

Apples dipped in honey, to symbolize the sweetness of the New Year. In addition, we eat challahs that are round, to remind us of the ongoing cycle of the year.

Yom Kippur

What

Day of Atonement

Why

Described in the Torah as a day to afflict our souls, and as a day that is to be considered the "Sabbath of Sabbaths."

When

Ten days after Rosh Hashanah. Mid-September to early October.

Symbols and Practices

- Fasting: No food or drink for the entire duration of the day.
- Kol Nidrei: First service on Yom Kippur, which leads off with the eponymous text. It's actually a legal declaration written in Aramaic in which we preemptively nullify all vows that we make in the coming year but won't be able to fulfill.
- The Book of Life: A continuation of the theme from Rosh Hashanah. On this day, however, the book is sealed, hopefully with our names inscribed inside.
- Jonah: This story of a reluctant prophet is read during the afternoon service. It is linked to this day because of its theme of repentance, atonement, and our ability to change God's decree with our sincere actions. Kids love the man-eating whale.
- *Vidui*: The congregation stands up together and recites a text listing sins and transgressions. Rather than being a specific set of actions performed by individuals, the *Vidui* symbolizes the collective ability of people to sin and harm others.
- Wearing white: It's traditional for the cantor, and sometimes others, to wear white throughout the day's services, as a sign of purity and starting over.

Let's Eat

Yeah, you wish.

Sukkot

....

What

One of the Three Pilgrimage Festivals. *Sukkot* means "booths."

Why

The Torah tells us to build and live in booths for the duration of the festival in order to remember that the Israelites lived in these temporary structures while they wandered in the desert.

When

Five days after Yom Kippur. Late September to late October.

Symbols and Practices

- *Sukkot*: These are the booths that we build. If we don't have our own, then it's common for a synagogue to have one for communal use. We should at least make the effort to eat as many meals as possible within its rickety walls. The *sukkot* also remind us that everything that we have, and all that protects us, comes from God.
- Lulav and etrog: The four species mentioned in the Torah—they comprise myrtle, willow, palm, and citron fruit. We hold these items together and wave them in all directions to show God's omnipresence.
- Connection to harvest: Sukkot includes symbols and themes of harvest. We also include a series of prayers called *Hoshanot*, which ask for God's salvation, tied in with the need for rain and a successful harvest.

Let's Eat

There are no specific traditional foods. We should eat as often as possible inside the *sukkah* (weather permitting).

Shemini Atzeret

What

Eighth day of assembly

Why

The Torah instructs us to have one more holy day on the eighth day after Sukkot.

When

The eighth day of Sukkot (which is a seven-day festival)

Symbols and Practices

- Prayer for Rain: Shemini Atzeret is when we get very serious about needing rain in order to survive. We've been leading up to this major prayer with themes of the harvest throughout Sukkot.

Let's Eat

There are no traditional foods associated with Shemini Atzeret. We may still eat in the *sukkah* but are not obligated to do so.

Simchat Torah

What

Rejoicing with the Torah

Why

Simchat Torah is never mentioned in the Torah, but it was created and popularized around the fifteenth century.

When

The second day of Shemini Atzeret

Symbols and Practices

- Finishing and restarting the cycle of Torah reading: We read the last chapters of the Torah and immediately turn back to the beginning and read the first words of Genesis. This symbolizes our enthusiasm for the Torah, and that our study of Torah is never completed.
- Dancing and singing: We treat Simchat Torah as a huge party—taking every Torah scroll out of the ark and dancing with them around the sanctuary.

Let's Eat

Apples, as a nod to Rosh Hashanah, and symbolizing that we're closing out this long period of holidays. Often the apples are candied or dipped in chocolate, to further symbolize the sweetness of the Torah, and to paint more of a contrast with Rosh Hashanah.

Chanukah

What

Festival of Lights

Why

To commemorate the Maccabees' unlikely victory over the Greeks in taking back control and then rededicating the Holy Temple. We remember the miracle of a one-day supply of oil lasting for eight full days.

When

Late November to late December

Symbols and Practices

- The Menorah: We light candles each night of Chanukah, adding one candle each evening.

- The Miracle: This story actually came hundreds of years after the events of Chanukah. It focuses the theme of the holiday on God and deemphasizes the military aspect.
- The Dreidl: A spinning top that has been connected with Chanukah for centuries.
- Presents: A more recent addition to the holiday's rituals, almost certainly because of its proximity to Christmas. Still, gifts of *gelt* (money) have been traditional for centuries.

Let's Eat

Latkes (potato pancakes). In Israel, jelly doughnuts. These foods are traditional because they're fried in oil, helping us to remember the miracle.

Purim

What

A minor holiday that recalls the defeat of the Jews' enemy, Haman. Purim means "lots," because Haman chose the date for his dastardly plan at random.

Why

We remember the events surrounding Esther, Mordechai, Haman, and Achashverosh, as recorded in the scroll of Esther.

When

Late February to late March

Symbols and Practices

- The *Megillah*: Literally, "scroll." We read the entire story of Esther and are instructed to hear every word.

- Noisemakers: During the reading, we use *groggers* or any other noisemaker to drown out the name of Haman whenever it is read.
- *Mishloach manot*: Exchanging food portions. It's traditional to send each other at least a couple of different kinds of foods.
- Gifts to the poor: We are also instructed to give to those in need.
- Dressing in costume: This is especially fun for the kids, but adults are encouraged to do so as well.
- *Purimspiel*: Some kind of play, skit, or other performance, where members of the congregation act out parts of the Purim story or simply make fun of the day's themes.

Let's Eat

Hamantashen—pastries in the shape of a triangle with a filling of some kind.

Passover

What

The second of the Three Pilgrimage Festivals. Also known as the Festival of Spring, and the Festival of Our Liberation.

Why

It recalls all the events surrounding the Israelites' time of slavery in Egypt, the rise of Moses, God's defeat of Pharaoh and Egypt, and the Exodus.

When

Spring. Late March to mid-April.

Symbols and Practices

- Seder: On the first two nights, we tell the story of Passover. There is a seder plate that we put on the table, which contains specific items that remind us of different aspects of the holiday.

- *Haggadah*: This is the book that we use at the seder.
- Matzah: We eat unleavened bread to remember that our ancestors fled Egypt in haste and didn't have time to let their dough rise.
- *Maror*: We also eat bitter herbs (often horseradish) to symbolize the bitterness of the Israelites while they were slaves in Egypt.
- The Four Questions: Recited at the seder, traditionally by the youngest person present. They set the tone for how we are supposed to teach the Passover story to each generation.

Let's Eat

Most significantly, matzah for the entire week of the holiday. In addition, there are many traditional foods eaten at the seder, including *karpas*, a green vegetable to symbolize spring; *charoset*, a mixture of apple, nut, and wine that symbolizes the mortar that the slaves used; and *maror*, a bitter herb often represented by horseradish.

Throughout the festival, we aren't allowed to consume any grains or leavened products.

Shavuot

What

The third of the Three Pilgrimage Festivals. Also known as the Feast of Weeks because it occurs exactly seven weeks after Passover.

Why

To commemorate God's giving the Torah to the Jews.

When

Mid-May to early June

Symbols and Practices

Not much to see here.

In ancient times, people would bring their first fruits to the Temple as an offering to God. This is a short, two-day festival.

Tikkun: It's traditional to study for all or part of the night before Shavuot as a demonstration of our willingness to accept the Torah all over again.

Let's Eat

Dairy foods are traditional. This might include cheese blintzes for dinner and cheesecake for dessert.

Tisha B'av

What

The ninth day of Av, a fast day

Why

To remember the tragic events surrounding the destruction of both Temples in Jerusalem.

When

Summertime. Mid-July to early August.

Symbols and Practices

- Fasting: Just like on Yom Kippur. We are not supposed to eat or drink anything for the entire duration.
- Mourning: We engage in rituals of mourning by not bathing (except as necessary), putting on nice clothes, or doing anything fun. We're not even allowed to study Torah.
- *Eichah*: The book of Lamentations. This book chronicles the horrible aftermath of the Temple's destruction, and we read it in services.

Let's Eat

Weren't you paying attention?

APPENDIX II

YOUR QUICK AND HANDY GUIDE TO ALL THE JEWISH MONTHS

HERE IS A quick listing of all the months in the Jewish calendar, the holidays that occur in each month, and how they correspond to the civil calendar.

Tishrei

When

September–October

What Holidays and Occasions

- Rosh Hashanah
- Fast of Gedaliah (minor fast)
- Yom Kippur
- Sukkot
- Shemini Atzeret
- Simchat Torah

Cheshvan

When

October–November

What Holidays and Occasions

None. This month is sometimes referred to as *Marcheshvan*, meaning "the bitter month of Cheshvan," because it contains no Jewish holidays.

Kislev

When

November–December

What Holidays and Occasions

- Chanukah (begins at end of month)

Tevet

When

December–January

What Holidays and Occasions

- Chanukah (conclusion)
- Tenth of Tevet (minor fast)

Shevat

When

January–February

What Holidays and Occasions

- Tu Bishevat

Adar[1]

When

February–March

What Holidays and Occasions

- Fast of Esther (minor fast)
- Purim

Nisan

When

March–April

What Holidays and Occasions

- Fast of the Firstborn (minor fast)
- Passover
- Omer Period (beginning)
- Yom HaShoah

---

1. During a Jewish leap year, an entire extra month is added to the Jewish calendar, to make sure that the Hebrew dates stay connected with the proper months in the civil calendar. When this happens, an extra month of Adar is added, so that we have Adar I and Adar II. In a leap year, the Fast of Esther and Purim fall in Adar II.

Iyar

When

April–May

What Holidays and Occasions

- Omer Period (continuing)
- Yom Hazikaron
- Yom Ha'atzma'ut
- *Lag B'Omer*

Sivan

When

May–June

What Holidays and Occasions

- Omer Period (conclusion)
- Shavuot

Tammuz

When

June–July

What Holidays and Occasions

- Seventeenth of Tammuz (minor fast)

Av

When

July–August

What Holidays and Occasions

• Tisha B'av

Elul

When

August–September

What Holidays and Occasions

No holidays, but in preparation for Rosh Hashanah, the shofar is blown at the conclusion of each weekday morning service.

APPENDIX III

GLOSSARY OF TERMS AND PHRASES

Aliyah (pl. *aliyot*): The honor of being called up to the Torah.

Chametz: Any leavened food that may not be consumed or used in any way on Passover.

Chanukiyah: The formal name for the nine-branched menorah used on Chanukah.

Chol HaMoed: The non-sacred intermediate days in the middle of Sukkot or Passover.

Conservative: A branch of Judaism that follows traditional Jewish law but has made changes over the years to reflect modern society.

Days of Awe: Rosh Hashanah and Yom Kippur. Also called the *High Holidays*.

G'lilah: The honor of dressing the Torah at the conclusion of the Torah service.

Grogger: Noisemaker used on Purim.

Haftarah (sometimes *Haftorah*): The reading from one of the books of the Prophets that is linked to that week's Torah portion.

Hagbah: The honor of lifting the Torah at the conclusion of the Torah service.

Haggadah: The book of texts, prayers, and blessings that is used at a Passover seder.

Halachah: The body of traditional Jewish law.

Hallel: A specific set of Psalms that is recited as a unit during services for certain Jewish holidays.

High Holidays: Rosh Hashanah and Yom Kippur. Also called the *Days of Awe*.

Kaddish: A prayer, written in Aramaic, that praises God and appears in the service numerous times and in different forms. The most well-known version is the Mourners' Kaddish, recited after the death of a family member.

Kashrut: The set of laws and instructions for keeping kosher.

Kittel: A white robe worn by the cantor and/or rabbi during Yom Kippur and other special times of the year.

Knesset: The Israeli Parliament.

Kohen Gadol: The high priest who was in charge of the Holy Temple.

Machzor: Prayer book that is used only on the High Holidays.

Megillah: Scroll. Sometimes used to refer to the book of Esther.

Midrash: A body of commentary on the Bible consisting of stories, legends, and other texts.

Mishnah: A major collection of Jewish law and the basis for the Talmud.

Mourners' Kaddish: See Kaddish.

Musaf: "Additional service." It mostly has to do with animal sacrifices that used to be offered in ancient Temple times.

Nisan: The first month of the Jewish year as written in the Torah. It contains the Festival of Passover.

Orthodox: The branch of Judaism that strictly follows traditional Jewish law.

Parsha: The selection of Torah that is read on any given Shabbat.

Prophets: The section of the Bible that follows the Torah. This section comprises books that tell us all about the ancient Israelite prophets and their messages.

Reform: The most liberal branch of Judaism, which does not believe that all traditional law is binding on today's Jews.

Rosh Chodesh: The first day of the Jewish month. Sometimes referred to as the New Moon.

Septuagint: The original Greek translation of the Tanakh.

Shabbat: The Jewish Sabbath.

Shalosh Regalim: The Three Pilgrimage Festivals—Sukkot, Passover, and Shavuot.

Shammash: The extra candle that is lit each night of Chanukah.

Shevarim: One type of shofar blast. Three short sounds.

Shoah: The Holocaust.

Shul: Synagogue.

Tallit (or *Tallis*): Prayer shawl worn during services.

Talmud: Volumes of Jewish teaching and discussion written two thousand years ago when the Jewish people were living in Babylonia.

Tanakh: The Jewish Bible. The word itself is an acronym that stands for the three sections of the Bible: Torah, Prophets, and Writings.

Tashlich: Ceremony performed on the afternoon of Rosh Hashanah, when people symbolically cast their sins away by tossing crumbs of bread into a body of water.

Tefillin: Small, black leather boxes and straps that are worn on the arm and head during a weekday morning service.

Teki'ah: One type of shofar blast. One long sound.

Temple: When written with a capital *T*, it refers to the Holy Temple that stood in Jerusalem about two thousand years ago and was the center of Jewish worship.

Teshuvah: Repentance.

Tishrei: The first month of the Jewish calendar.

Torah: The first section of the Jewish Bible, consisting of the Five Books of Moses.

T'ruah: One type of shofar blast. Nine very short sounds.

Tzedakah: Charity.

Tzitzit: The fringes that are attached to each of the four corners of the tallit.

Vidui: Prayer of confession that is recited on Yom Kippur.

Writings: The third section of the Bible, which contains Psalms, Proverbs, Esther, and other later books.

Yahrzeit: The anniversary of the day in the Jewish calendar on which a family member died.

Yizkor: The memorial service recited four times a year: on each of the Three Pilgrimage Festivals and on Yom Kippur.

INDEX

Midrash, *114*
Mishnah, 6, 78
music (*nusach*), *30*, 53, *62*, 88–91

Omer, 159–69; and agricultural calendar, 159–60; counting of, 160–62; important days of, 163–68; meaning of, 159; prohibitions during, 162–63; in Torah, 159
Orthodox Judaism, 152, 165, *166*

Passover, 109–34, 135, 136, 137, 138, 142–43, 159, 160, 169, *175*, 177; in Jewish calendar, 6; kosher for, 118–19, 122; meaning of, *125*, 134, 161; Prayer for Dew, *62*, 133–34; preparation for, 118–22; in Torah, 110–17; traditional foods, 123–24, 125–27, 131–32. *See also* seder
Purim, 93–107, 177; charity, 106; drinking on, 102, 104; meaning of, 105–6; noisemakers, 101–2; services, 101–2; *spiel*, 104, *105*; traditional foods, 106–7

Reform Judaism, 9, 60, 70, *174*
repentance, 11–15, 25–26, 35, 36–37, 61
Rosh Hashanah, 5–23, 25–26, 27, 51, 54, 61, *125*, 142, 158, 170, 176; and agricultural calendar, 7; Book of Life, 20–21, 23; in Jewish calendar, 6, 8–9; meaning of, 5, 11–15, 19, 23; pagan roots of, 7–8; in Torah, 6; traditional foods, 22, 71
Ruth, book of, 133, 143–45. *See also* Shavuot

Sanhedrin, 8
seder, 109; Four Questions, 124–27; *Haggadah*, 122, 124, 125, 128–31, 132; meaning of, 122; symbols, 123–24

Shavuot, 135–49, 160; and agricultural calendar, 136, 137, 148; in Jewish calendar, 136–37; kosher for, 147–48; meaning of, 135, 142, 148–49; in Torah, 136, 138–42; and Torah study, 146, 148–49; traditional foods, 146–47
Shema, 60, 68, 133, *174*
Shemini Atzeret, 57–64, 70, 71; and agricultural calendar, 59–60, 61–62; in Jewish calendar, 58; meaning of, 58, 71; Prayer for Rain, 60–62, 70, 133–34; in Torah, 58, 71
shevarim. See shofar
Shoah. *See* Holocaust
shofar: blasts, 19–20; connection to Rosh Hashanah, 16, 17; on Shabbat, *19*
Simchat Torah, 57–58, 59, 64–71; dancing with the Torah, 65, 66, 69; in Jewish calendar, 64; meaning of, 59, 64, 67, 71; traditional foods, 71
Song of Songs, 133, 143. *See also* Passover
sukkot (booths), 41, 42; building of, 43–45, 46; decorations, 44–45, 47; living in, 45–46, 62
Sukkot (festival), 41–56, 58, 135, 136, 137, 142, 160; and agricultural calendar, 52; in Jewish calendar, 41, 42–43; meaning of, 41, 56; pagan roots of, 47–52, 54; in Torah, 42, 52

Talmud, 78, 85, 155, 162, 165, *173*
tashlich, 21–22
teki'ah. See shofar
the Temple, 37–38, 42, 43, 60, 75–76, 78, 80, 81, 83–84, 89, 110, 123, 152, 153–55, 156, 159, 165, 169, 171, 176, 177. *See also* Tisha B'av
teshuvah. See repentance
Three Pilgrimage Festivals, 42, 54–55, 63, 66, 110, 133, 136, 139,

ABOUT THE AUTHOR

CANTOR MATT AXELROD has served Congregation Beth Israel in Scotch Plains, New Jersey, for over twenty years. A native of the Boston area, he is a graduate of Brandeis University and the Jewish Theological Seminary of America. Cantor Axelrod is a past member of the Executive Council of the Cantors Assembly and a former president of its New Jersey region, and he has served on the United Synagogue Council on Jewish Education.

Cantor Axelrod is the author of *Surviving Your Bar/Bat Mitzvah: The Ultimate Insider's Guide*. He is also an avid aviation enthusiast and a licensed pilot and flight instructor. Cantor Axelrod lives in New Jersey with his wife and two sons.